PRAISE FOR
21st CENTURY POINT AND FIGURE

"Mr du Plessis has taken traditional Point and Figure charts and successfully integrated key momentum indicators, volume and other commonly used tools, bringing Point and Figure analysis into the 21st century. As a market technician who has used Point and Figure for 20 years, I strongly believe that there is no better time to educate yourself on these updated approaches, first to better navigate the 'noise' that is bound to persist in all types of markets, and second to be able to effectively expand your horizons of market observation across the globe. With such high reliability, and a uniquely objective and quantifiable nature, there is no charting technique like Point and Figure, and this book can guide you to mastery of it."

Craig Johnson, CFA, CMT / Senior Technical Market Strategist, Piper Jaffray / President, Market Technicians Association

"Du Plessis brings Point and Figure into the modern era with new insights and innovation to enhance this time-proven technique. This work is invaluable to the serious chartist and highly recommended for the professional tasked with forecasting price targets or establishing risk management strategy. It pushes the envelope for Point and Figure enthusiasts to help them use their skill in new ways."

Gordon Scott, Managing Director, CMT Program, Market Technicians Association

"Jeremy du Plessis has been teaching Point and Figure charting on the Society of Technical Analysts (STA) Diploma Courses for nearly a quarter of a century. In 2005 he decided to write *The Definitive Guide to Point and Figure: A Comprehensive Guide to the Theory and Practical Use of the Point and Figure Charting Method*, which has been on the STA's reading list ever since. His new book, *21st Century Point and Figure*, takes Point and Figure charting to a whole new level. It expands on his first book and includes invaluable new techniques, such as advanced analysis of relative strength and spreads, market breadth and indicators on Point and Figure charts, to name but a few. The STA is pleased to add *21st Century Point and Figure* to its Diploma Course reading list."

Axel Rudolph, Chairman of the Society of Technical Analysts

"Once again Jeremy du Plessis has pushed the boundaries of Point and Figure charting by applying moving averages and Bollinger Bands in unique ways to the chart. His application of time based indicators makes the Point and Figure chart even more relevant to today's traders and investors."

Bruce M. Kamich, CMT, Adjunct Professor of Finance at Baruch College / Past President of the Market Technicians Association and the Market Technicians Association Educational Foundation

"An expert in Point and Figure technique, Mr du Plessis is well qualified to take Point and Figure into the 21st century. Although it touches on the background of Point and Figure, this is a more advanced book, full of practical information. Picking up where *The Definitive Guide to Point and Figure* left off, Mr du Plessis explains a variety of innovative techniques that truly do bring Point and Figure into the modern age."

Ken Tower, CMT

21st Century
Point and Figure

21st Century
Point and Figure

New and Advanced Techniques for

Using Point and Figure Charts

By Jeremy du Plessis

Hh

HARRIMAN HOUSE LTD

18 College Street

Petersfield

Hampshire

GU31 4AD

GREAT BRITAIN

Tel: +44 (0)1730 233870

Email: contact@harriman-house.com

Website: www.harriman-house.com

First published in Great Britain in 2015

Paperback ISBN: 9780857194428

eBook ISBN: 9780857194619

British Library Cataloguing in Publication Data

A CIP catalogue record for this book can be obtained from the British Library.

To Angelique and Daryl

About the Author

Jeremy du Plessis, CMT, FSTA, trained as an automotive engineer, then an economist, but gave them both up to become a Technical Analyst. In 1983 he founded Indexia Research and pioneered the development of PC-based technical analysis software with the Indexia range of technical analysis systems. During the 1980s he developed a number of technical tools and indicators under the banner of Indexia, such as the Indexia Market Tracker and Indexia moving averages, which are still used in software to this day.

He is an expert on Point and Figure charts, and the Indexia software was the first PC-based system to draw them correctly and clearly in the early 1980s. He lectures the Point and Figure module for the Society of Technical Analysts and sets the Point and Figure syllabus for the International Federation of Technical Analysts. He has taught Technical Analysis, and in particular Point and Figure, to thousands of professional traders and investors over the last 30 years. In 2001, after running Indexia Research for nearly 20 years, he agreed to merge the company with Updata Ltd, where he is now head of Technical Analysis and Product Development, and the designer of the Updata PC and smartphone technical analysis software.

He is a Fellow of the Society of Technical Analysts (FSTA) in the UK, and a member of the American Market Technicians Association (MTA) as well as the American Association of Professional Technical Analysts (AAPTA). He is a holder of the Chartered Market Technician (CMT) designation awarded by the MTA.

Acknowledgements and Thanks

I would not be in this business were it not for my late brother Dennis, together with whom the Indexia name was invented and the Indexia company formed in 1981, and who then encouraged me to spin off Indexia Research Limited to produce and sell PC-based Technical Analysis software. I did this together with my new business partner and programmer, John Johnson, who worked with me to produce the finest Point and Figure charts and to computerise log scale Point and Figure when no one considered it possible. The Indexia Research Market Analyser software we produced was the true leader in technical analysis and in particular Point and Figure charts up to 2001, when the company merged with Updata Limited.

Writing this book would have been impossible without the charts from the software produced by Updata's amazing development and coding team, who are responsible for the best Technical Analysis system available today.

I am indebted to three people for their valuable comments and technical advice: Jeanette Young for reading my initial draft to see if it made sense and was worth publishing; Tony Smith who had the unenviable task of reading through the final draft, producing pages of advice, comments and demands for more clarity from me; and Craig Pearce, my editor at Harriman House, who corrected my grammar and helped restructure many of the paragraphs to read correctly. I can't thank them enough for their devotion and enthusiasm. Their input has made the book a far better one.

Finally my thanks go to my wife, Lynne, who endured my constant ramblings about a new book and encouraged me to complete it. This book is dedicated to my children, neither of whom will read it, but of whom I am very proud.

As usual, any errors are my own.

Jeremy du Plessis

Berkhamsted, United Kingdom 2015

Any comments on the book will be gratefully received at **PointandFigure@indexia.com**

Preface

This is an advanced book on Point and Figure charting. It is a comprehensive guide to those Point and Figure techniques that can be regarded as 21st century innovations. As any new technique takes time to develop, some of the ideas presented here were first suggested, although not fully developed, before the turn of the century and were therefore introduced in my previous book, *The Definitive Guide to Point and Figure*. They are, however, included here in their entirety, so this is a complete guide to 21st century Point and Figure analysis.

This book assumes that you are familiar with traditional Point and Figure techniques – either through the daily use of Point and Figure charts, or through having read a good text on the subject – and want to look at new ways to use Point and Figure charts. Although the first chapter is a quick refresher on Point and Figure, it can't cover every aspect of the method with respect to terminology, construction, patterns, trend lines and targets. If you are not familiar with these aspects of Point and Figure, you are urged to read either *The Definitive Guide to Point and Figure* or another book on the subject, as this will give you the grounding required to fully appreciate the advanced techniques in *21st Century Point and Figure*.

The new techniques described here open up a whole world of new analysis tools for Point and Figure charts and address most of the deficiencies claimed by detractors of the method.

STRUCTURE OF THIS BOOK

Chapter 1 – Quick Refresher on Point and Figure

This chapter is designed for those who have not used Point and Figure before, or those who need a reminder of the basics. It gives a quick run down of where Point and Figure charts came from and how they are constructed. It explains the terminology used, how patterns are formed, and how trend lines and targets are used with Point and Figure charts. It is not a comprehensive guide to traditional Point and Figure techniques so if after reading it you are still unsure, it is recommended that you read a more basic text before continuing with the advanced 21st century techniques.

Chapter 2 – 21st Century Chart Construction

This chapter discusses two additional ways to construct Point and Figure charts using the end of period summary of open, high, low and close. Both give a different perspective and bias when drawing the charts. It also introduces a mathematical way to determine Point and Figure box sizes, instead of guessing them, and how to convert these into log scale box sizes.

Chapter 3 – Moving Averages on Point and Figure Charts

This chapter explains how to construct and draw moving averages on Point and Figure charts. It then describes a number of ways to use them.

Chapter 4 – Using Other Tools on Point and Figure Charts

This chapter expands on the use of moving averages to identify trend, by explaining how to construct and use Donchian channels, Bollinger bands and Parabolic SAR on Point and Figure charts.

Chapter 5 – Indicators of Point and Figure Charts

This chapter explains how time-based indicators like MACD, RSI and others can be used with Point and Figure charts to improve the analysis.

Chapter 6 – Volume on Point and Figure Charts

This chapter explains how vertical column volume and horizontal at price volume can be incorporated into the analysis of Point and Figure charts.

Chapter 7 – New Point and Figure-based Techniques

This chapter introduces a new indicator based on 45° trend lines which may be used on Point and Figure as well as time-based charts. It also explains how to translate 45° lines on to time-based charts.

Chapter 8 – Advanced Analysis of Relative Strength and Spreads

This chapter shows how to construct Point and Figure charts of relative strength and shows how using Point and Figure enhances the analysis of relative strength and spreads.

Chapter 9 – 21st Century Market Breadth

This chapter explains the existing Point and Figure-based market breadth indicator and introduces two new ones which sit on either side of it in time horizon.

TECHNICAL ANALYSIS SOFTWARE AND DATA

I have used the Updata software to create the charts for this book. As the person responsible for the design and development of the software, I know that it offers everything a Point and Figure analyst needs, quickly and, more importantly, accurately.

One of the problems introduced when technical analysis became computerised is that it only takes one person to program an incorrect method for users to accept it and others to follow it, presuming it is correct. The result is that what is wrong becomes accepted as right. Point and Figure has not been immune to this and so there are a lot of inaccurate Point and Figure charts out there, so beware.

Most of the data used to produce the charts comes from Bloomberg LP, the world's premier source of good, accurate data. In addition, I have also used Updata's real-time data feed for energy and foreign exchange data.

I have used daily time series as well as a variety of intraday time frames. Weekly is never used with Point and Figure, and although the only true Point and Figure charts are those using tick data, the lack of availability of reasonable tick histories prevents its use. In any case, 1 minute data is an adequate substitute for tick data.

Contents

Introduction

A T THE START OF THE 21st CENTURY, POINT AND FIGURE HAD BEEN around for over 120 years, with almost no change to the original concept. It started off as a tick-by-tick charting system and although ways to use different data series were eventually found, the technique has remained unchanged. In some ways it is good that it has stood the test of time and that the method is just as effective now as it was in the 19th and 20th centuries, but that does not mean that we should not push the frontiers and look at modifications, improvements and new features in Point and Figure charts that are enabled by modern technology. These need to be done without altering the framework on which Point and Figure was built, of course.

As a charting technique, Point and Figure stagnated for 100 years until the early 1980s, coming in for criticism even from committed Point and Figure chartists. During this time the development of other charting techniques continued, while Point and Figure analysis consisted of essentially Point and Figure patterns, subjective and 45° trend lines, and Point and Figure targets. The lack of time on their charts persuaded Point and Figure chartists that there was nothing else they could add to their method; it meant that any time-based tools such as moving averages and indicators could not be used. Lack of volume was another of the main criticisms levelled at Point and Figure as it meant that the importance of any column could not be determined, which in turn meant that Point and Figure signals could not be assessed on their validity.

The advent of the personal computer in the early 1980s had a number of effects on Point and Figure charts. Although some technical analysts persisted with hand-drawn charts, others moved on to those drawn using the PC. The problem at the time was that most PC charting programs did not have Point and Figure charts, so many analysts abandoned the method. Those who found software that was able to draw Point and Figure charts correctly employed some lateral thinking, which allowed development of the approach to accelerate.

Besides simply allowing anyone to draw a Point and Figure chart without an intimate knowledge of construction, the PC allowed true log scale charts to be drawn, as well as the automation of the manual tasks of drawing 45° trend lines and the establishment of Point and Figure targets. Furthermore, in the 1990s, the ability to draw moving averages on Point and Figure charts, lost for decades, was reintroduced and popularised and this showed that further development of Point and Figure could be undertaken, not just for the sake of doing something different, but rather because there was great benefit to be had.

This book will cover the use of moving averages on Point and Figure charts, explaining new ways to read them. It will also cover the use of the Parabolic SAR, Donchian channels and Bollinger Bands, as well as the use of well-known calculated indicators such as RSI, MACD and others.

In addition, new tools and indicators based entirely on Point and Figure are also introduced. Different ways of incorporating volume, previously considered persona non grata on Point and Figure charts, are introduced as well. Computers have also allowed more scientific calculation of box sizes to be developed, as well as other ways of constructing charts using an end of period summary rather than tick data.

Traditionally, Point and Figure has contributed only one indicator to the study of market breadth, but in the second edition of *The Definitive Guide to Point and Figure* two new indicators were proposed and these are included here as well, because they are 21st century innovations. Together, all these concepts and ideas will prepare you for using Point and Figure in the 21st century.

Although this book is about more advanced techniques, it is important to understand that these techniques do not preclude the need for the more traditional patterns, trend lines, targets, etc. Trend lines, particularly 45° on 3-box charts, still play a very important part in the analysis of Point and Figure charts and you will see them used extensively here.

Which instruments work best with Point and Figure?

There is no restriction on the instruments that can be drawn as Point and Figure charts. The charts work equally as well with indices, ETFs, equities, bonds, interest rates, futures, commodities, currencies or any other series of data. I could have used a different instrument for each chart in the book, but instead I have chosen just a few and used them throughout the book to make comparisons of different techniques easier.

No set of charts can satisfy every reader, so it is recommended you blank out the names when inspecting the charts as it does not matter what market and what instruments you are interested in – the analysis is the same. Remember, too, that Point and Figure is useful for both short-term and long-term analysis. The patterns and the way the charts behave is the same no matter what time horizon is used.

Point and Figure terminology

I use standard Point and Figure terminology throughout the book, which is consistent with the terminology used in *The Definitive Guide to Point and Figure*. I use the term **box size** to refer to the value of each X and O. I use the word **arithmetic** to describe a Point and Figure chart where the box size is the same across the whole chart and is measured in points, $, £, €, cents, pence, etc. I use the word **log** to describe a Point and Figure chart where the box size is a percentage and therefore the points value of box sizes varies across the chart. I use the word **reversal** to refer to the number of boxes required to change from X to O and vice versa. I use **1-box reversal**, or just **1-box**, to refer to the original Point and Figure charts that require the reversal of one box to change from X to O or O to X. I use **3-box reversal**, or just **3-box**, to refer to charts where a reversal of three boxes is required to change from X to O or O to X. I use the words **time-based** to refer to charts where time is measured along the x-axis. Any other terminology is discussed in Chapter 1.

Chapter One. Quick Refresher on Point and Figure

ALTHOUGH YOU SHOULD REALLY READ A GOOD TEXT ON traditional Point and Figure techniques before attempting this book, this chapter is a quick refresher for those who need a reminder. Obviously it can't cover every aspect, but it should provide you with sufficient knowledge to understand the concepts covered in this book.

DEVELOPMENT OF POINT AND FIGURE

The first thing to note about Point and Figure charts is that they do not have a time scale. The chart does not advance along the x-axis as time passes, but rather it does so as intermediate trends change and new columns are built.

The method started off as a price recording system where traders would write down the prices traded throughout the day in columns; a rising column of numbers to denote rising prices and a falling column of numbers to denote falling prices. After a while they began to notice patterns in their price record and so what started off as a price recording system became a charting method known as a 'Figure chart'.

As writing down numbers became tedious, some replaced the numbers with Xs and the chart became known as a 'Point chart'. Figure charts and Point charts existed together and traders referred to their 'Point' charts and their 'Figure' charts, or their 'Point and Figure' charts, the name used today. Figure charts eventually ceased to be used in the late 1930s, and in the late 1940s a new plotting method was developed using Xs for the rising columns and Os for falling columns. Figure 1-1 shows the development of the Point and Figure method. It should be noted that Point charts still tend to be used in certain circumstances to this day.

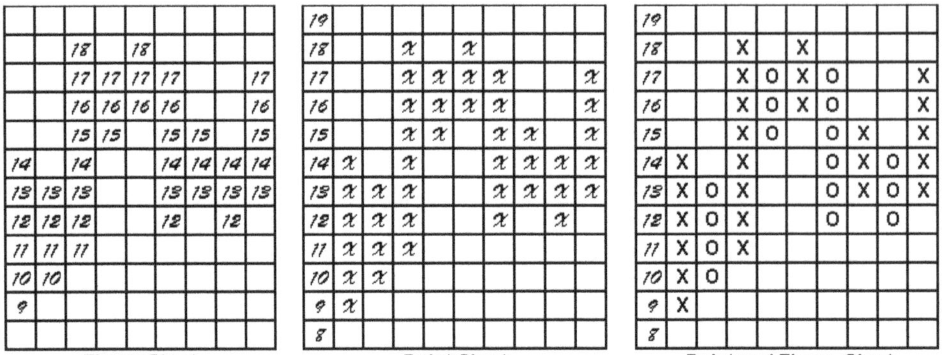

Figure Chart

18		18					
17	17	17	17			17	
16	16	16	16			16	
15	15		15	15		15	
14		14	14	14	14		
13	13	13		13	13	13	13
12	12	12		12		12	
11	11	11					
10	10						
9							

Point Chart

19								
18		𝑥		𝑥				
17		𝑥	𝑥	𝑥	𝑥			𝑥
16		𝑥	𝑥	𝑥	𝑥			𝑥
15		𝑥	𝑥		𝑥	𝑥		𝑥
14	𝑥	𝑥			𝑥	𝑥	𝑥	𝑥
13	𝑥	𝑥	𝑥		𝑥	𝑥	𝑥	𝑥
12	𝑥	𝑥	𝑥		𝑥		𝑥	
11	𝑥	𝑥	𝑥					
10	𝑥	𝑥						
9	𝑥							
8								

Point and Figure Chart

19								
18		X		X				
17		X	O	X	O			X
16		X	O	X	O			X
15		X	O		O	X		X
14	X		X			O	X	O	X
13	X	O	X			O	X	O	X
12	X	O	X			O		O	
11	X	O	X					
10	X	O						
9	X							
8								

FIGURE 1-1: THE DEVELOPMENT OF THE POINT AND FIGURE CHART

POINT AND FIGURE CONSTRUCTION

To construct a Point and Figure chart, a single value, called the box size, must be assigned to each square on the chart. A box size of 1 means that as the price rises or falls by 1 point or more, new squares are filled. Any price change less than 1 point is, however, ignored. This can be seen in Figure 1-1 above. The box size is not always 1 point and depends on the price of the instrument and how sensitive you want the chart to be. For example, you may use a box size of 100 for the Dow, but a box size of 0.01 for the euro. Once a box size has been determined for any instrument, reducing it increases the sensitivity of the chart and therefore reduces the time horizon. Increasing it obviously reduces the sensitivity and increases the time horizon.

The plotting column changes direction, from X to O or O to X, when the price reverses by a prescribed number of boxes. The original method, still used today, is the 1-box reversal chart, where a reversal in price by the value of at least one box changes the direction of the plotting column.

With this method it is important to note that it is possible to have an X and an O in the same column because if the price reverses by one box only, say from X to O, and then reverses again from O to X, a change of column is not required for the second reversal because there is space to write the X in the current O column. This is called one-step-back and can be seen in Figure 1-2. It is important for the analysis of 1-box reversal charts that the one-step back has an X and O in the same column, because it affects the width of the chart and therefore trends and targets. It is a common plotting error for a new column to be started each time.

As 1-box reversal charts were quite sensitive, a more condensed version, called a 3-box reversal chart, was also used. These were constructed and transcribed from the 1-box reversal charts. With 3-box reversal charts, the price must reverse by at least the value of three boxes before changing columns and can therefore never have an X and O in the same column. 3-box reversal is now the most popular Point and Figure method used today for reasons of objectivity in analysis.

Figure 1-2 shows a 1-box and 3-box construction using the same data set. Notice the X and O occurring in the same columns in the 1-box chart. Notice too how much more sensitive the 1-box chart is. 1-box charts provide more detail and, in effect, look inside the 3-box chart.

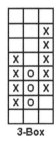

FIGURE 1-2: 1-BOX AND 3-BOX REVERSAL CHARTS

The parameters of a Point and Figure chart are the box size and reversal and the charts are therefore named according to these. So a chart drawn using the 3-box reversal method where the box size is 10 is called a 10 x 3 Point and Figure chart; one where the box size is 5 using the 1-box reversal method is called a 5 x 1.

Point and Figure charts where the box size is a points, $ or cents value are called arithmetic charts, but it is also possible to draw log scale Point and Figure charts, where the box size is a percentage. This means that each box is a percentage of the price at that level, for example 1%, and the value of each box above is 1% larger, and each below is 1% smaller. As prices rise, therefore, the value of the boxes grows exponentially. The advantage of this is that the sensitivity – the price divided by box size – is constant throughout the chart, whereas as with arithmetic charts the sensitivity increases as the price rises. A log scale 1-box reversal chart where the box size is 1% is named as a 1% x 1 Point and Figure chart.

Point and Figure charts were traditionally drawn using each price as the instrument traded, but lack of availability of this tick data eventually led Point and Figure analysts to construct their charts using a single daily price, either the close at the end of the day or the high or low[1] at the end of the day. The construction method chosen depends on a number of factors, namely time horizon, volatility and sensitivity. It is also possible to use interval data, such as 1 minute, 5 minute, hourly, etc., and take either the close or the high or low at the end of every time interval. These charts constructed using interval data are now preferred over Point and Figure charts drawn with tick data because of the availability of long histories of intraday interval data.

---

1 The rules as to whether the high or the low is used are detailed in *The Definitive Guide to Point and Figure*.

The time horizon of a Point and Figure chart depends primarily on the box size, and to a lesser extent on the underlying data being used. As mentioned earlier, the smaller the box size, the more sensitive the chart to price movements and consequently the shorter the time horizon. Typically, a Point and Figure analyst will look at two, perhaps three, Point and Figure charts of the same instrument with different box sizes to obtain a clearer picture of what is happening.

Point and Figure construction on a squared grid, with data placed into boxes, allows objective application of tools and therefore objective analysis. 3-box reversal charts, more so than 1-box, are best used for this, making them a favourite amongst modern Point and Figure chart users.

The interpretation of 3-box charts is more objective because the patterns are more defined, with fewer variations than those in 1-box charts. Consequently patterns can be uniquely identified. Essentially all signals from Point and Figure charts are based on breakouts and in 3-box charts these are easier to see.

POINT AND FIGURE SIGNALS

A basic Point and Figure buy signal occurs when a column of Xs rises above the previous column of Xs, called a double-top buy; a sell occurs when a column of Os falls below the previous column of Os, called a double-bottom sell. Figure 1-3 shows these two basic Point and Figure patterns.

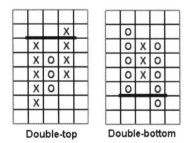

Double-top   Double-bottom

FIGURE 1-3: DOUBLE-TOP BUY AND DOUBLE-BOTTOM SELL

The strength of any Point and Figure pattern depends on the pattern's width. The more columns it takes before the breakout, the stronger the subsequent signal. So a triple-top or triple-bottom (neither shown) lead to a stronger signal than the double equivalent.

In Point and Figure pattern analysis, reassertion of control is important for determining the pattern's strength. In any pattern, the bulls are in control when there is a column of Xs, and the bears are in control when there is a column of Os. Reassertion of control occurs when a pattern switches from being bull controlled to bear controlled and back again. Conversely it could be bear to bull and back again.

The most common example of this is the catapult pattern, which has a number of components. For a bullish catapult to occur, there must be a triple-top breakout, followed by a pullback into the pattern – although not deep enough to trigger a sell signal – which is then reversed, resulting in a double-top breakout. Although the pullback does not result in a signal in the opposite direction, it is sufficient to shock the bulls who must either capitulate or reassert their control of the pattern. The fact that, in spite of being rebuffed, a group can regain control is important for the pattern's strength. See Figure 1-4 for the bullish and bearish versions of the catapult.

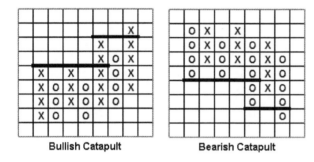

FIGURE 1-4: BULLISH AND BEARISH CATAPULTS

Many other Point and Figure patterns have been identified and named, and you should familiarise yourself with these. Not every breakout is taken as a buy or sell – Point and Figure analysts look to see if it is part of a bigger pattern, but also they take note of trend lines.

TREND LINES AND TARGETS

Point and Figure analysts have traditionally drawn 45° trend lines on 3-box reversal charts and subjective trend lines on 1-box reversal charts, although subjective lines can also be drawn on 3-box charts. The advantage of the 45° lines is that they are drawn alternately from tops and bottoms without the need for a second touch point. They therefore objectively define whether the chart is bullish or bearish and help to validate Point and Figure signals. Once the 45° trend line is drawn, price touches on it strengthen the line. This is shown in the uptrend in Chart 1-1, which is a log scale 1% x 3 chart of the S&P 500 with objective 45° trend lines.

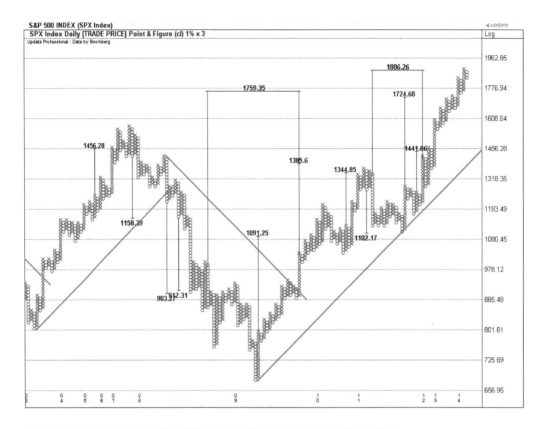

CHART 1-1: S&P 500 1% X 3 POINT AND FIGURE CHART WITH 45° TREND LINES AND TARGETS

The ability to obtain targets from a Point and Figure chart is an important part of Point and Figure analysis. Targets are based on thrusts from highs and lows as well as the width of congestion areas. Chart 1-1 shows a number of targets based on these. The calculation of these targets is complex if the chart is log scaled, as with Chart 1-1.

* * *

You will have noted in reading this refresher that there is a lot to understand about Point and Figure charts before you can use them effectively, so once again it is recommended that you read *The Definitive Guide to Point and Figure* or another good text if you are at all unfamiliar with Point and Figure charting.

Chapter Two. 21st Century Construction

INTRODUCTION

THE USE OF COMPUTERS TO DRAW POINT AND FIGURE CHARTS HAS allowed Point and Figure analysts to push the frontiers of chart construction. Not only did true log scale charts become possible in the 1980s, but in the 2000s box sizes can be determined by mathematical formulas instead of by feel and experience. Charts based on intraday interval or daily data can now be constructed using various combinations of the close, high, low and open, instead of the limited choice of close or high-or-low.

Before looking at what the 21st century has brought, it is important to understand the position in the 20th century.

20TH CENTURY BOX SIZES

When Point and Figure charts were first drawn, box sizes were set to ½ or 1 point, because that catered for every instrument being charted at the time. But as stock and commodity prices increased during the 20th century, box sizes had to increase to cater for the higher prices, so box sizes of 2, 5 or 10 started to be used. Those box sizes were still applied to the whole chart, no matter by how much the price had changed over time. Eventually, however, Point and Figure analysts realised that one box size could not cater for the whole price range, and that the box size had to increase as the price increased.

It was decided, therefore, to change the box size at certain price levels. So some arbitrary rules were devised, such as below 20 the box size is ½ a point, from 20 to 100 it is 1 point, between 100 and 500 it is 2 points, and so on. This made Point and Figure construction difficult, the validity of trend lines suspect and targets difficult to calculate if they crossed these threshold levels, but it did allow better charting of instruments with large price ranges.

This method, now called the 'traditional' method by some, is outdated and should no longer be used because computers can handle it far more accurately. What these 'traditional' chartists were trying to do by increasing the box size at certain levels as the price increased was to keep the percentage change in price required to generate a new box more or less constant throughout the chart; a sort of log scaling without doing the calculations. Unfortunately, the percentage change was not constant because the box size changed in steps at various price levels.

The introduction of the IBM PC in the early 1980s changed everything because it allowed more complex calculations to be undertaken. Log scaling of time-based charts was easily handled, but it was thought impossible with Point and Figure charts because they are built on a squared grid. However, it was not long before it was realised that Point and Figure charts could be drawn on a true log scale by making the box size a percentage instead of a points value.

In 1984 Indexia Research Ltd released a new version of its Market Analyser software with true log scaled Point and Figure charts, where a percentage box size allowed a smooth increase and decrease in points value of the box as the price increased and decreased. This has become the standard for drawing long-term Point and Figure charts and, as you will see, it is essential when applying modern tools to Point and Figure charts. The reason is that the sensitivity of the chart remains the same, no matter what level the price is at, and the transition from one level to the next is smooth. The calculation for constructing log scaled charts may be found in *The Definitive Guide to Point and Figure*.

Before you can draw a Point and Figure chart, you have to specify the box size, which, up until now, was either 'guessed' based on experience, or estimated by setting the points box size to a percentage of the latest price or range of prices.[2]

Although time horizons are difficult to define for everyone, the table below sets out the percentages that should be used to determine box sizes. It is split into daily data and intraday data, the reason being that if you keep reducing the box size on daily charts, the chart will eventually become unreadable with long columns of Xs and Os. This is the signal to switch to interval data which could be hourly, 5 minute, 1 minute, or any intraday time frame. Charts constructed with multiple prices per day allow smaller box sizes to be used and that means shorter time horizons.

DAILY DATA

Long term	2%
Medium to long term	1%
Medium term	0.50%
Short to medium term	0.25%

INTERVAL DATA

Medium to short term	0.25%
Short term	0.10%
Very short term	0.05%

TABLE 2-1: PERCENTAGES USED TO DETERMINE BOX SIZES FOR DAILY DATA AND INTERVAL DATA

---

2 Although a percentage of the last price is the most common, you will find that for some instruments, typically bonds, a percentage of the price range gives a better estimate of the box size.

The percentages in the tables can either be used to estimate the points box size by multiplying the percentage by the price, or as the percentage box size to draw a log scaled chart. You may wish to adjust the percentages down for currency charts.

21st CENTURY BOX SIZES

However you look at it, the percentages in the table above are guesswork based on experience. The good news is that in the 21st century, box sizes can be determined mathematically instead of by guesswork.

Box sizes based on volatility

Instead of basing box sizes on the price level or the price range over the chart, they can be based on volatility. This is because there is a direct link between the sensitivity of the Point and Figure chart and the volatility of the underlying data. The more volatile the price, the larger the box size needs to be, so calculating box sizes based on volatility is a more scientific way of establishing the correct size for the instrument you are studying. There are many ways to calculate volatility and any calculation may be used, but the two formulas used here are standard deviation and Average True Range (ATR).[3]

As with all volatility calculations, you must decide the number of periods over which the volatility is to be calculated. Ideally this should be based on the number of periods of data you intend to use to construct the Point and Figure chart. This effectively means that box sizes based on volatility tend only to be used for short-term charts, because the calculated box size may not apply outside the volatility period.

Of course there is no reason why you can't calculate a 260-day volatility and apply it to a daily Point and Figure chart showing one year of data, but anything further back than a year may not be applicable to the box size unless the price range is in the same area. However, you will recall that log scale charts adjust the box size to any price level, so having determined the points box size based on volatility, it is easy to convert that into a percentage box size for drawing log scale charts, as explained in the following sections.

Box size based on standard deviation

Standard deviation is one of the most popular statistical methods for calculating volatility. To calculate a box size based on standard deviation, you calculate the standard deviation for the data range you wish to study and then decide how many standard deviations you wish to take into account. With box sizes this would normally be less than 1 standard deviation, somewhere between 0.2 and 0.5.

---

3 Average True Range was devised by J. Welles Wilder in his 1978 book *New Concepts in Technical Trading Techniques*.

The number of standard deviations can be equated to your time horizon. The greater the number, the greater your time horizon. 0.5 standard deviations would give a box size of twice that of 0.25 and consequently twice the time horizon.

Chart 2-1 is a daily Point and Figure chart of the euro. The box size is 0.0058, which is 58 pips. It is based on a measure of 0.25 standard deviations over 260 days.[4] Normally when drawing a Point and Figure chart of the euro, box sizes of 100, 75 or 50 pips are used, so 58 is unusual, but it is an annual volatility-based box size. This would normally only be valid for the last year of data, but because the euro is in a similar range it can apply outside the year's range. However, even though the euro is in a range, the sensitivity of the chart at the top of the range is not the same as that at the bottom of the range. For this reason, a log scale box size can be used.

CHART 2-1: DAILY CHART OF EURO WITH 0.0058 BOX SIZE BASED ON 0.25 STANDARD DEVIATIONS OVER 260 DAYS

Having obtained the fixed box size based on volatility, it is possible to translate that into a percentage box size for a log scaled chart by dividing the box size determined from the standard deviation by the latest price or an average of a number of prices and multiplying by 100.[5] In this example the last price is 1.3920 and the average of the last 260 prices is 1.3425, so the percentage box size is 0.416% if the last price is used, or 0.432% if an average of 260 prices is used. This now allows a log scale chart to be drawn in order to analyse longer histories.

---

4 In Updata, the formula is 0.25*STDDEV(CLOSE,260).
5 100*(box size/last price) or 100*(box size/average of last prices).

Chart 2-2 is a log scaled Point and Figure with a box size of 0.416%. Notice that the last part of the chart is similar to, but not identical to, Chart 2-1 with a fixed box size of 0.0058. 45° trend lines have been added to both charts to help you to compare the shapes. The main difference is that the 0.416% box size means the points value adjusts as the price rises and falls, whereas the fixed 0.0058 box size is 0.0058 throughout the chart.

CHART 2-2: DAILY CHART OF EURO WITH 0.416% LOG SCALE BOX SIZE BASED ON 0.25 STANDARD DEVIATIONS OVER 260 DAYS

The calculation of box sizes is not limited to daily charts; they may be calculated for charts drawn using tick data or intraday interval data. The volatility of intraday data is, by definition, lower than that for daily data, so the box size is automatically adjusted to a lower value, which is what you want.

Chart 2-3 is a 1 minute chart of the euro, with a box size of 0.00023 or 2.3 pips, significantly smaller than the 58 pips used for the daily chart. It is based again on a 0.25 standard deviation calculated over 260 minutes instead of 260 days. This translates into a log scale box size of 0.016%, which is shown in Chart 2-4.

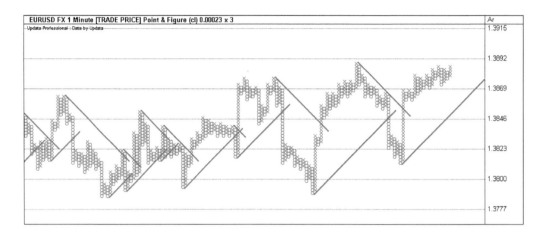

CHART 2-3: 1 MINUTE CHART OF EURO WITH 0.0023 BOX SIZE BASED ON 0.25 STANDARD DEVIATIONS OVER 260 MINUTES

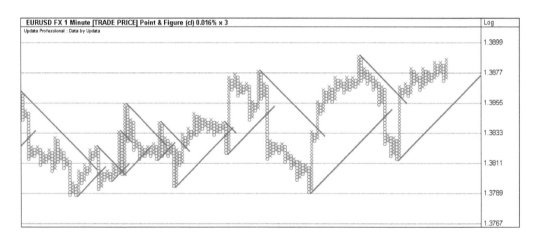

CHART 2-4: 1 MINUTE CHART OF EURO WITH 0.016% LOG SCALE BOX SIZE BASED ON 0.25 STANDARD DEVIATIONS OVER 260 MINUTES

This method is not restricted to specific instruments – the advantage of it is that it will calculate the best box size on any instrument or index you want without the need to know anything about the instrument.

Chart 2-5 is a daily chart of the S&P 500 with the box size calculated using 0.25 standard deviations over 260 days. The box size comes out as 18, which equates to a percentage box size of 1%. This is a typical medium to long-term box size.

CHART 2-5: DAILY CHART OF S&P 500 WITH 18 POINT BOX SIZE BASED ON 0.25 STANDARD DEVIATIONS OVER 260 DAYS

Using standard deviation as the basis to work out what box size to use is logical, because volatility and chart sensitivity are closely related. It removes some of the subjectivity, but you do still have to decide how many periods to take into consideration and how many standard deviations to apply. Once the box size has been calculated, you may then calculate the log equivalent.

Box size based on Average True Range (ATR)

ATR is a non-statistical calculation of volatility. It is the average of a number of periods of true range, where true range is the maximum amount the price has moved based on various measures of the range.[6] It is more closely related to Point and Figure box size determination than standard deviation-based volatility because it is based on the average amount price moves over the period selected, which is ideal for setting the box size.

Unlike box sizes based on standard deviation, you do not have to multiply ATR by a factor – the box size is simply the ATR value. This makes it less subjective. Moreover, you will find that adjusting the period of the ATR makes very little difference to the ATR value. J. Welles Wilder – the creator of ATR – used 14 periods, but 20 is often used.

---

6   See J. Welles Wilder's book, *New Concepts in Technical Trading Techniques*, for more details.

The box size of 17 in Chart 2-6 of the S&P 500 is based on an ATR of 20 days. Although not shown, the box size using an ATR of 260 days is 16, showing that there is little difference when changing the ATR period.

Think what the ATR box size means. It means that the average movement of the S&P over 20 periods is 17 points. That is exactly what you want the Point and Figure chart to isolate, so making the box size equal to 17 does just that. Notice, too, how well the 45° lines describe the trends, reinforcing the choice of box size.

CHART 2-6: DAILY CHART OF S&P 500 WITH 17 POINT BOX SIZE BASED ON 20 DAY ATR

The chart of the S&P ranges from 680 to 1870, which means that if a fixed box size of 17 is used for the whole chart, as in Chart 2-6, the sensitivity at the 680 level is very low. Sensitivity is defined as price divided by the box size at that level. This is the main reason for drawing log scale charts – to ensure constant sensitivity throughout.

As with standard deviation, therefore, the points box size obtained from ATR can be converted into a log scale box size by dividing the ATR box size of 17 by the current price of 1870 or an average of the last 20 prices, giving a box size of 0.9% to draw the log scale chart. The percentage box size makes the chart more valid over a longer period.

You will notice a marked difference in the shapes of the arithmetic Chart 2-6 and log scale Chart 2-7, although they are similar towards the end of the chart. The arithmetic chart applies the box size of 17 throughout the chart even when the S&P is at 680. That means at 680, the percentage box size is 2.5%, whereas it is 0.9% at the end of the chart, showing that the sensitivity of the chart is not constant and so patterns on the lower priced parts of the chart are invalid.

CHART 2-7: DAILY CHART OF EURO WITH 0.9% LOG SCALE BOX SIZE BASED ON 20 DAY ATR

As with standard deviation, the ATR value adjusts when the time frame of the data changes. The ATR for 1 minute or 5 minute data will be significantly less than that for daily data and consequently the box size will be smaller, which is exactly what you want and expect it to be. The reason is that the true range from one minute to the next is much smaller than that of one day to the next.

Chart 2-8 is a 5 minute chart of the S&P. The ATR box size is reduced to 1.1, meaning that the average range from one 5 minute period to the next is just over 1 point.

CHART 2-8: 5 MINUTE CHART OF S&P 500 WITH 1.1 POINT OX SIZE BASED ON 20 5 MINUTE ATR

Chart 2-9 is an hourly 1-box reversal chart of gold. The ATR box size is $3. Although the chart is drawn in the X only point chart style, the up Xs are coloured blue and the down Xs are coloured red to make it easier to see the large number of one-step backs. This shows that the $3 box size is exactly right for picking up the intraday movements of gold.

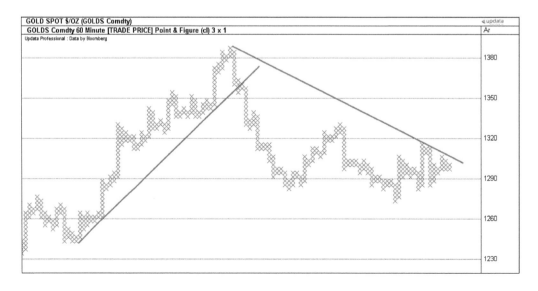

CHART 2-9: HOURLY 1-BOX REVERSAL CHART OF GOLD WITH 3 POINT BOX SIZE BASED ON 20 HOUR ATR

Two volatility measures have been proposed for determining the box size. Some will prefer standard deviation because of its roots in statistics, others will prefer ATR because it is rooted in the market and looks at the true range of prices. Either way, they both take the guesswork out of determining box sizes.

In order to pre-empt the question as to why a number of ATRs can't be calculated on different sections of the data to provide a number of different box sizes for the chart, you need to consider what that would mean. There is no reason why you can't obtain three ATR box sizes from three sections of the data, but having done that you can only use one of them. The reason is Point and Figure charts have no time scale, and data from two years ago, as in the case of the charts above, may actually be in the same price range as the data from one year ago. If the ATR box size from two years ago is different from the ATR box size from one year ago, it would be impossible to draw the chart because, at the same price level, there would be different box sizes represented by the same row of squares, which would become out of synchronisation as the price moves from one row to the next. This is why the only solution is to convert the ATR box into a percentage box size for a log scale chart.

Box sizes based on other formulas

Although basing box sizes on the recognised measure of volatility is a logical way to calculate the box size, there is almost no limit to the formulas you can now use. For example, you could set the box size to the square root of the latest price.[7] The box sizes determined from a square root tend to be larger and therefore give a longer-term time horizon, but once again you may adjust the time horizon by multiplying the square root by a factor.

Using the S&P 500 again in order to enable comparison with earlier charts, the square root of the last price in our example is 44 rounded to the nearest whole number, which equates to a percentage box size of over 2%.[8] This would be regarded as long term, so a factor needs to be applied to shorten the time horizon. Chart 2-10 is drawn using ¼ of the square root of the current price, which translates into a box size of 11.

The problem with this type of formula is that it does not adjust when intraday data is used because the time frame of the data has no bearing on the latest price (the latest price is always the same no matter what time frame is used). So a 1 minute chart of the S&P would also have a box size of 11 and that would be too big. One way around this is to calculate an average of the square roots of the last, say, 100 prices. This would be 100 daily prices if the data is daily and 100 one minute prices if the data is 1 minute, so it will yield a different box size for different time frame data.

You can see that choosing the right formula to calculate the box size is important. Ideally, it should be based on a series of prices rather than the last price because, as you have seen, the last price does not adjust for different time frame data.

---

7   In Updata, the formula is EXPBASE(CLOSE,0.5).
8   box size/last price *100

CHART 2-10: DAILY CHART OF S&P 500 WITH 11 POINT BOX SIZE BASED ON ¼ OF THE SQUARE ROOT OF THE LAST PRICE

Point and Figure charts compartmentalise the data into boxes so the move from one box to the next should reflect how the price of the instrument changes. The absolute change in price from one period to the next measures how the price moves, so taking an average of those changes is another good basis for a box size calculation.

Once again the S&P 500 is used so you have a direct comparison with earlier charts. The box size of 9 in Chart 2-11 is determined by taking a 20 day average of the absolute 1 day changes in price,[9] which in a way is a measure of volatility, but more importantly it defines the typical points change in the S&P 500. The 9 point box size translates into a log scale box of 0.47%, which is a shorter time horizon than produced by previous formulas.

All formulas must be based on price itself, rather than the result of another formula, because this would produce a box size unrepresentative of the price. For example, you should not base the box size on the RSI value because no matter what the price, the value of RSI will always be between 0 and 100.

---

9 In Updata, the formula is SGNL(ABS(CLOSE(1)-CLOSE),20,M).

S&P 500 INDEX (SPX Index)	update
SPX Index Daily [TRADE PRICE] Point & Figure (cl) 9 x 3	Ar
Updata Professional : Data by Bloomberg	

CHART 2-11: DAILY CHART OF S&P 500 WITH 9 POINT BOX SIZE BASED ON 20 DAY AVERAGE OF 1 DAY PRICE CHANGES

Throughout the 20th century, box sizes were estimated based on the knowledge of the instrument. Often analysts would have to draw a number of charts to find the box size that was best suited. Using a formula based on how the price moves takes away much of the guesswork and provides you with the best box size for the instrument you are looking at. This means you don't need prior knowledge of the instrument or its price.

Take a mid-cap South African stock like JD Group. Unless this is your market, you would not know its price or how it behaves, so it would be difficult to know what box size to use. Chart 2-12 is a 132 x 3 chart of JD Group. The box size was calculated using the 20 day ATR. Notice how good the chart looks and how well the 45° trend lines pick up the trend. It is unlikely you would have guessed 132, because it's equivalent to a 4.8% log scale box size.

CHART 2-12: DAILY CHART OF JD GROUP WITH A BOX SIZE OF 132 POINTS BASED ON 20 DAY ATR

21ST CENTURY CONSTRUCTION METHODS

When Point and Figure charts are constructed using tick data, every price is used so there are no alternative ways to use the data. However, if the chart is constructed using daily or intraday interval data, you are faced with four variables at the end of each period: open, high, low and close. For more than 50 years, either the close or the high/low[10] were used, but in the second decade of the 21st century two alternative ways to use the data were introduced. These are the low/high and open/high/low/close methods. Although these two methods were introduced in the second edition of *The Definitive Guide to Point and Figure*, they are discussed here again because they are very much a 21st century innovation.

Low/high method

The high/low method gives preference to the high or low depending on the direction of the current column. The high is given preference if the current column is an X column and the low is given preference if the current column is an O column, according to a set of rules. This effectively favours the direction of the current column, but you may wish to draw your chart by favouring the opposite direction instead, and that is where the low/high method comes in.

---

10   Either the high or the low is used according to a set of rules. It is not possible to use the high and the low because the order in which they occurred is unknown.

The rules for the low/high method are opposite to those for the high/low method, as follows:

» Take note of the direction of the current column. Is it an X or O column?

» If the column is X, look at the low to see if it produces a reversal.

    » If it does, change columns and plot a new column of Os, ignoring the high.

    » If the low does not produce a reversal, look at the high to see if a new X can be plotted. If so, plot the X and ignore the low.

    » If the low does not produce a reversal and high does not produce a new X, no new plot is recorded.

» If the column is O, look at the high to see if it produces a reversal.

    » If it does, change columns and plot a new column of Xs ignoring the low.

    » If the high does not produce a reversal, look at the low to see if a new O can be plotted. If so, plot the O and ignore the high.

    » If the high does not produce a reversal and the low does not produce a new O, no new plot is recorded.

This is essentially a more conservative method than the high/low method; it is always looking for a column change before looking for a continuation of the column.

Figures 2-1 and 2-2 show a chart constructed with the high/low and low/high methods respectively, using the same table of prices.

276								X
275	X							X
274	X	O					X	X
273		O					X	O	X
272		O					X	O	X
271		O					X	O	X
270		O			X		X	O
269		O			X	O	X
268		O			X	O	X
267		O	X		X	O	X
266		O	X	O	X	O
265		O	X	O	X
264		O	X	O	X
263		O		O
262				

High	Low
274	273
275	268
274	267
269	268
268	263
266	264
267	265
266	263
268	265
270	267
269	266
269	267
271	268
274	271
274	272
272	270
276	272

FIGURE 2-1: CHART CONSTRUCTED USING THE HIGH/LOW METHOD

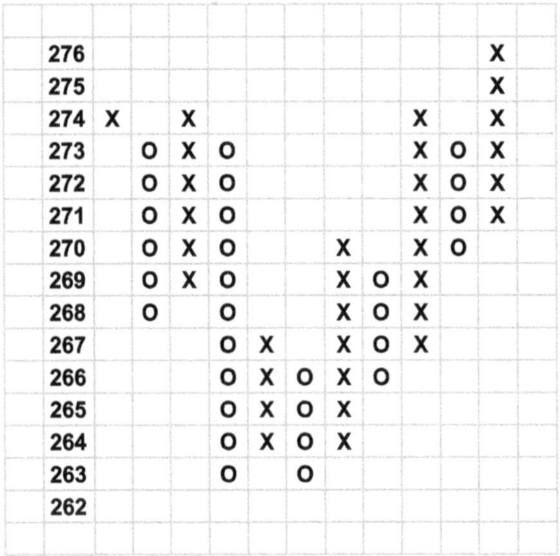

	1	2	3	4	5	6	7	8	9
276									X
275									X
274	X		X				X		X
273		O	X	O			X	O	X
272		O	X	O			X	O	X
271		O	X	O			X	O	X
270		O	X	O		X	X	O	
269		O	X	O	X	O	X		
268		O		O	X	O	X		
267			O	X	X	O	X		
266			O	X	O	X	O		
265			O	X	O	X			
264			O	X	O	X			
263			O		O				
262									

High	Low
274	273
275	268
274	267
269	268
268	263
266	264
267	265
266	263
268	265
270	267
269	266
269	267
271	268
274	271
274	272
272	270
276	272

FIGURE 2-2: CHART CONSTRUCTED USING THE LOW/HIGH METHOD

As you can see, favouring the reversal leads to more column changes and therefore wider patterns in the low/high method in Figure 2-2, but it depends on the range between high and low. You will see that although the reversal is favoured, there are a number of occasions where there has been a continuation of the column, because on each occasion the price in the opposite direction has not been 3 boxes away to result in a reversal.

Favouring the reversal will also lead to more 45° trend changes because of the wider patterns, however, you will be surprised to learn that the differences between high/low and low/high charts are not as marked as you might expect. The differences are more noticeable with smaller box sizes and in fact with larger box sizes you may not see any differences with your eye. The reason is that as the box size increases, so the price change required for a reversal becomes larger and so the countertrend reversal does not occur often.

CHART 2-13: DAILY HIGH/LOW CONSTRUCTED CHART OF COMCAST CORP. WITH BOX SIZE OF 0.25%

Chart 2-13 is a daily high/low chart of Comcast Corp. with a short to medium-term box size of 0.25%. Chart 2-14 is the low/high version. Immediately you can see that the shape of the two charts is different. If these were 1% charts, however, you would not see any difference at all.

Notice that the high/low Chart 2-13 has remained in an uptrend with the price well above the bullish support line, whereas the low/high Chart 2-14 has changed trend a number of times, with the 45° trend lines hugging the data. Notice that, in general, the columns of Xs and Os are shorter in the low/high chart, making the chart more readable than the high/low chart. The shorter columns indicate that favouring of reversals leads to more column changes. Remember, when the columns become too long, charts become difficult to interpret. The remedy is to shorten the time frame of the data so the chart can be drawn with more than one price per day.

CHART 2-14: DAILY LOW/HIGH CONSTRUCTED CHART OF COMCAST CORP. WITH BOX SIZE OF 0.25%

Changing from 3-box to 1-box reversal yields the same result. Chart 2-15 and Chart 2-16 show 1-box reversal high/low and low/high charts respectively. Once again, the low/high chart has shorter columns even though the price change to continue in the same column is the same as that to change columns. Moreover, subjective trend lines drawn on the low/high chart describe the trends better than those on the high/low chart. The readability of the high/low chart is once again affected by longer columns.

CHART 2-15: DAILY 1-BOX REVERSAL HIGH/LOW CONSTRUCTED CHART OF COMCAST CORP. WITH BOX SIZE OF 0.25%

CHART 2-16: DAILY 1-BOX REVERSAL LOW/HIGH CONSTRUCTED CHART OF COMCAST CORP. WITH BOX SIZE OF 0.25%

Switching to intraday interval data, keeping the box size the same as the daily charts above, shows little difference between high/low and low/high charts, as shown in the hourly Chart 2-17 and Chart 2-18. If you look carefully there are differences, but not as marked as they are in the daily charts. Although not shown with chart examples, reducing the box size again shows up more differences.

CHART 2-17: HOURLY HIGH/LOW CONSTRUCTED CHART OF COMCAST CORP. WITH BOX SIZE OF 0.25%

CHART 2-18: HOURLY LOW/HIGH CONSTRUCTED CHART OF COMCAST CORP. WITH BOX SIZE OF 0.25%

Open/high/low/close method

One of the problems with drawing Point and Figure charts on daily (or interval) data is being faced with an open, high, low, close summary at the end of the period, but not knowing the sequence in which the high and low occurred. For this reason, in the past only one price per day has been used, either the close or the high-or-low, as you have seen, thus avoiding the need to know the sequence.

The open/high/low/close (ohlc) method uses the open, high, low and close in the order defined by a set of rules based on assumptions about the path the price has taken during the day. The issue is really only about whether the high or low occurred first because the open is obviously the first price and the close is clearly the last price of the period.

If the close and open are not equal, then the rules are straightforward and as follows:

» If close > open, the sequence is open, low, high, close.

» If close < open, the sequence is open, high, low, close.

If, however, the close equals the open, then there are a number of sequences:

» If close = open = high = low, there is no sequence, just the single price is used for the day.

» If close = open = low, the sequence is open, high, close. The low is ignored because it is equal to the close.

» If close = open = high, the sequence is open, low, close. The high is ignored because it is equal to the close.

» If close = open and is below the middle of the high/low range, the sequence is open, high, low, close.

» If close = open and is above the middle of the high/low range, the sequence is open, low, high, close.

On rare occasions it is possible that close = open and is exactly the middle of the high/low range. In this situation:

» If the current column is an X column, the sequence is open, high, low close.

» If the current column is an O column, the sequence is open, low, high, close.

As you can see, the rules result in either 1, 2, 3 or 4 prices per day being used to construct the chart. 2 prices are used when open = low and close = high or open = high and close = low. The rules can result in an X and an O being plotted per day, whereas the close, high/low and low/high methods result only in an X or an O, never both.

Figure 2-3 shows a chart constructed using the ohlc method from the same table of prices as was used in Figures 2-1 and 2-2 , but this time with the open and close price included. The shape is different from both the high/low and low/high methods and the chart is the widest of the three because more than one column can be plotted per day.

													Open	High	Low	Close
276											X		273	274	273	274
275	X								X		X		274	275	268	268
274	X	O	X					X		X	O	X	268	274	267	268
273		O	X	O				X	O	X	O	X	268	269	268	268
272		O	X	O				X	O	X	O		268	268	263	264
271		O	X	O				X	O	X			265	266	264	265
270		O	X	O		X		X	O				265	267	265	266
269		O	X	O		X	O	X					266	266	263	266
268		O		O		X	O	X					266	268	265	267
267			O	X		X	O	X					267	270	267	269
266			O	X	O	X	O						269	269	266	267
265			O	X	O	X							267	269	267	269
264			O	X	O	X							269	271	268	271
263			O		O								271	274	271	274
262													274	274	272	272
													272	272	270	272
													275	276	272	275

FIGURE 2-3: CHART CONSTRUCTED USING THE OHLC METHOD

Chart 2-19 is a 0.25% x 3 ohlc chart of Comcast Corp., so you can compare it with high/low Chart 2-13 and low/high Chart 2-14. Immediately you can see that the patterns are wider in the ohlc chart because in many cases more than one column is being plotted per day.

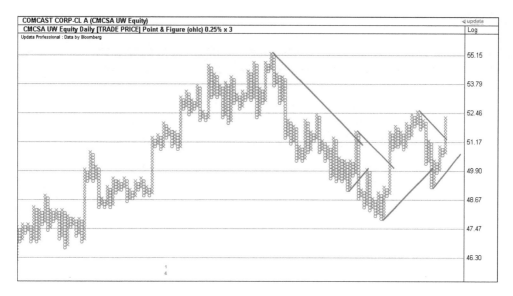

CHART 2-19: DAILY OPEN/HIGH/LOW/CLOSE CONSTRUCTED CHART OF COMCAST CORP. WITH BOX SIZE OF 0.25%

You should not lose sight of why the ohlc method is required. It is there as a substitute for using intraday data in the hope that it will mimic a chart drawn with intraday data where the path during the day is known. Although it is better to use intraday data, it is not practical to draw, say, a 5 or 10 year chart based on 1 minute or 60 minute data, which is where a daily chart constructed with ohlc data would be used.

Chart 2-20 is a 1 minute 0.25% x 3 chart of Comcast Corp. constructed using the close at the end of every minute. Because it is constructed in this way, the path between the high and low is known exactly. Now compare 1 minute Chart 2-20 with daily ohlc Chart 2-19. They are very similar, indicating that the ohlc method used on daily data is a good approximation for a chart constructed with intraday data.

CHART 2-20: 1 MINUTE CLOSE CONSTRUCTED CHART OF COMCAST CORP. WITH BOX SIZE OF 0.25%

SUMMARY

It was not until the early 1980s that true log scale charts became available. Prior to that, Point and Figure analysts arbitrarily changed the box size at certain intervals to achieve a pseudo log scale. That method, now called the 'traditional method', no longer has a place in the 21st century. To draw true log scale charts the box size is set to a percentage so that the value of the box varies exponentially as the price rises and falls. These log scale charts are vital for longer-term analysis and for drawing various indicators on Point and Figure charts, covered in later chapters.

Whether you are drawing charts using fixed or variable box sizes, in the past it was always a guess as to what box size to use, based on experience. That is no longer the case – the 21st century has provided ways to estimate box sizes mathematically using formulas which can then be converted to log scale percentage box sizes.

Although almost any formula may be used, it makes sense to consider formulas based on volatility, rate of change and alternative scaling. Formulas based on absolute price alone are best avoided as these do not adjust when the periodicity of the data is changed, because the last price is always the same.

It is recognised that there are many ways to calculate volatility, but only two methods have been considered; one from statistics and one from technical analysis. Standard deviation is a popular statistical way to calculate volatility and, in doing so, allows more accurate box sizes to be calculated based on a multiple of the standard deviation of the data under consideration. Average true range (ATR), however, comes directly from Technical Analysis and like standard deviation allows box sizes to be determined in a more scientific way.

Two other proposals of formulas to calculate box sizes have been put forward. The first is to simply take a multiple of the average square root of a series of prices and the second is to take an average of the price changes from one period to the next. The average of price changes is directly related to how the price of the instrument moves. It also means that intraday data will yield a different box size from daily data because the price move from one period to the next is different. There is, however, no doubt that this is just the start of scientific box calculation. In the coming decades it is likely that better formulas will be devised, as those covered here are by no means the only ones.

Of the two volatility methods, ATR is favoured for two reasons. The first is, unlike standard deviation, no subjective multiplier is required because ATR is based on absolute price changes. The second is that the ATR value does not change significantly if the period of the data under consideration changes.

The 21st century has brought two new construction methods, meaning that there are now four ways to use summary end of period data to construct the chart. Tick data will always be the best way to construct a Point and Figure chart, but there are a number of reasons why tick data is no longer the only way. Long tick histories are virtually impossible to obtain and manage, which means that end of period summary data needs to be used. Adding more ways to handle construction using end of period data may be seen as complicating an already complicated construction process, but the computer allows the parameters to be changed so quickly that it is not an issue. What you have to do is narrow down your choices.

The close only method is a logical method that uses the close at the end of every time frame, whether daily, hourly, 1 minute, etc. When used with daily data it provides a longer-term view given all the other parameters are the same. When used with intraday data it does provide a price path through the day. Critics of the close only method with daily data complain that it takes no account of the day's range, and so to combat this the high/low method was devised in the mid-20th century. Now there is also the low/high method, which places the emphasis on reversals rather than continuation of the column.

There is little to choose between the high/low and the low/high methods when larger box sizes are used, but with smaller box sizes you will find the low/high method has shorter column lengths and describes the trends better than the high/low method and so should be favoured. And on that basis, the high/low method can now be discarded, because there is no difference when larger box sizes are used and the low/high is better when smaller box sizes are used. Finally, there is the ohlc method, which when used with daily data mimics an intraday chart because it attempts to define the path the price has taken during the day by using four pieces of price information – the open, high, low and close. It should be favoured where no intraday data is available or when a shorter-term view than that provided by daily data is required.

Chapter Three. Moving Averages on Point and Figure Charts

INTRODUCTION

THE USE OF MOVING AVERAGES ON POINT AND FIGURE CHARTS IS not a 21st century technique. The technique was first made public when David Upshaw, who was at Drexel Burnham Lambert at the time, published an article on it in the February 1979 Market Technicians Association (MTA) *Journal of Technical Analysis*, where he credited Gilbert Foster with its invention in the 1960s.

However, because Point and Figure charts were at the time drawn by hand, calculating the moving averages on them was a lengthy process, so the technique never caught on until Kenneth Tower reintroduced it in a chapter on the subject in *New Thinking in Technical Analysis*, edited by Rick Bensignor, in 2000.

The lateral thought that the length of a moving average could be measured in columns rather than time periods is what allowed moving averages to be drawn on Point and Figure charts. Although not strictly a 21st century technique, the ability to draw moving averages is the one thing that has given Point and Figure the momentum to become the favoured method of the 21st century.

The key to drawing moving averages is the understanding that Point and Figure charts are not one-dimensional as many believe, but two-dimensional, where the first dimension is price on the y-axis and the second dimension is number of columns on the x-axis. These columns represent intermediate changes in direction. On non-Point and Figure charts, the second dimension is time and is used as the parameter to calculate moving averages. So to draw moving averages on Point and Figure charts you must average per column rather than per time period.

CONSTRUCTING A MOVING AVERAGE ON A POINT AND FIGURE CHART

It is important to understand that a moving average *on* a Point and Figure chart is a moving average *of* a Point and Figure chart and not of the raw data, as is the case with time-based charts. So before you can draw a moving average on a Point and Figure chart, you have to first draw the Point and Figure chart, then construct the moving average from that chart.

For this to work effectively, the moving average must be consistent throughout the chart, which means that the sensitivity of the Point and Figure chart must remain the same at every price level. The only way to ensure that is to draw true log scale[11] Point and Figure charts where the box size is a percentage rather than a number of points. This is something that Foster and Upshaw were unaware of at the time they were working, as their charts were arithmetic with a fixed box size. Making the box size a percentage allows the points value of the box to adjust to the price level. Of course it is possible to draw a moving average on fixed box size arithmetic charts, but these should only be used for short-term charts or if the chart's range is small, so as not to warrant a box size change.

If this is confusing, take the Dow Jones Industrial Average Index for example. In 1981 it was around 1000. That means to obtain a medium-term view, a box size of 10 would have been used. In 2013, however, the Dow was around 12,000, making a box size of 10 far too sensitive. In this case, to obtain a medium-term view a box size of 100 would need to be used. But if that same box size was used to produce a chart on the 1981 data, it would amount to a move of 10% to plot a new box and 30% for a reversal, so the earlier part of the chart would be of no use and consequently moving averages calculated and drawn on the early part of the chart would be of no use either. Log scale charts based on percentage box sizes ensure that no matter which part of the chart you are looking at, and no matter what the price, the sensitivity is the same.

Point and Figure charts advance along the x-axis, not as time passes, but as columns change from up-columns to down-columns, from Xs to Os, or Os to Xs. So the length of any moving average is measured in columns rather than days, weeks or minutes as is the case with line, bar or candle charts. The question is – what price per column must the moving average be based on? You can't base it on the last price in the column, because the last price is always the highest X or lowest O in any column and that would have a zigzag effect. Foster decided that each column should be assigned a single proxy price which is the midpoint of each column. For example, where a column runs from 130 to 210 the midpoint is (210+130)/2 = 170.

Once the proxy value for each column has been determined, a moving average of any column length may be calculated across the chart using the midpoint of each column and then calculating a moving average in one of the many standard ways; simple arithmetic, exponential, weighted, etc. There are no restrictions on the moving average calculation.

---

11 See *The Definitive Guide to Point and Figure*, chapter 2, for a full description and the calculation of log scaled Point and Figure charts.

Chart 3-1 shows a 1% x 3 Point and Figure chart of the S&P 500 with a 1 column simple moving average. This is a unit length moving average so it connects the proxy prices, i.e. the midpoint of each column. It is therefore the 'raw' data on which Point and Figure moving averages are calculated.

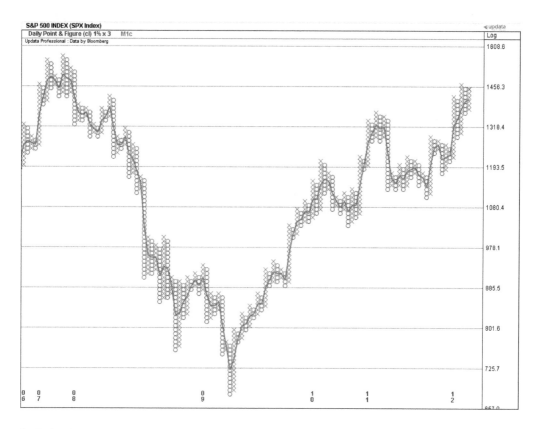

CHART 3-1: 1% X 3 OF S&P 500 WITH 1 COLUMN MOVING AVERAGE

Chart 3-2 shows the same 1 column moving average but with the Point and Figure chart removed so you can see how the centre proxy value of each column traces out.

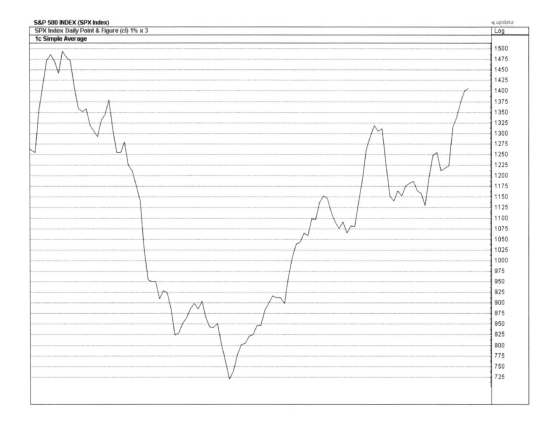

S&P 500 INDEX (SPX Index)

SPX Index Daily Point & Figure (cf) 1% x 3

1c Simple Average

CHART 3-2: 1 COLUMN MOVING AVERAGE OF A 1% X 3 POINT AND FIGURE CHART OF THE S&P 500

The line in Chart 3-2 is what the Point and Figure chart has been reduced to for the purpose of calculating moving averages, so a 20 column moving average of this line is a 20 column average of the Point and Figure chart itself. Chart 3-3 shows a 20 column moving average of the 1 column moving average, which is the same as the 20 column moving average on the Point and Figure chart in Chart 3-4.

It is important to emphasise that the moving average is dependent on the Point and Figure chart and the way it is constructed. A 20 column moving average drawn on a close only Point and Figure chart will be different from one drawn on a high/low chart and different again from one drawn on a 1-box reversal chart for the simple reason that the length and number of columns will be different. Similarly, changing the box size and reversal will result in a different looking Point and Figure chart and consequently a different looking moving average.

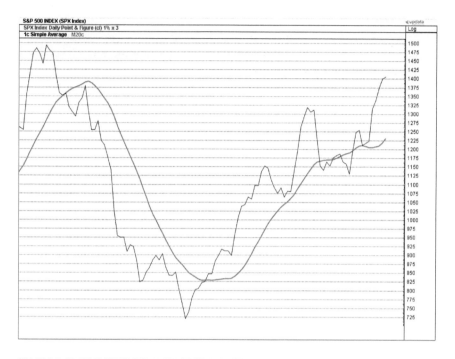

CHART 3-3: 20 COLUMN MOVING AVERAGE OF THE 1 COLUMN MOVING AVERAGE OF THE 1% X 3 POINT AND FIGURE CHART OF THE S&P 500

CHART 3-4: 1% X 3 CLOSE ONLY POINT AND FIGURE CHART OF THE S&P 500 WITH A 20 COLUMN MOVING AVERAGE

Chart 3-4 showed a 20 column moving average on a 3-box close only constructed chart, whereas Chart 3-5 shows a 20 column moving average on a high/low constructed chart. The moving averages are the same length but are different shapes because the underlying Point and Figure charts are different.

CHART 3-5: 1% X 3 HIGH/LOW POINT AND FIGURE CHART OF THE S&P 500 WITH A 20 COLUMN MOVING AVERAGE

Changing the reversal also changes the chart and consequently the moving average. Chart 3-6 is a 2-box reversal chart. Compare it with Chart 3-4 and you will see that the change in reversal from 3 to 2 has obviously changed the chart and consequently the moving average.

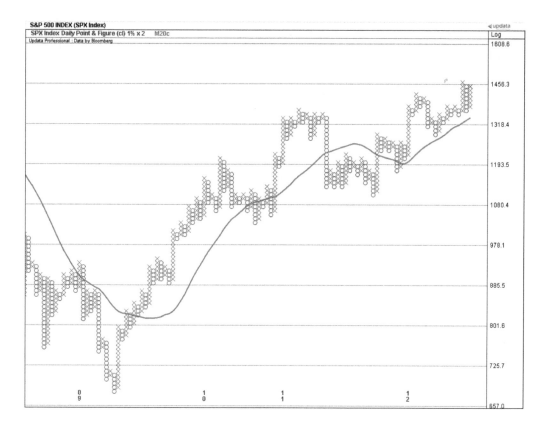

CHART 3-6: 1% X 2 CLOSE ONLY POINT AND FIGURE CHART OF THE S&P 500 WITH A 20 COLUMN MOVING AVERAGE

Moving averages may also be used on 1-box reversal charts. Even though there can be an X and O in the same column, the calculation is the same. Chart 3-7 is a 1% x 1 chart of the S&P 500 constructed on the close price with a 20 column moving average. It is worth spending some time comparing it to Chart 3-4 and Chart 3-6.

CHART 3-7: 1% X 1 CLOSE ONLY POINT AND FIGURE CHART OF THE S&P 500 WITH A 20 COLUMN MOVING AVERAGE

Moving averages may also be drawn on intraday interval charts, as shown in Chart 3-8, which is a 1 minute 0.125% x 3 chart of the S&P 500.

CHART 3-8: 1 MINUTE 0.125% X 3 CHART OF THE S&P 500

Of course, changing the box size will also have a dramatic effect on the chart and moving average, as will changing the time frame of the data. This does make the use of moving averages on Point and Figure charts more complex but the rule is to draw the chart first and then add the moving average to help your analysis of the chart you have drawn, and not to try to alter the Point and Figure construction parameters to suit the moving average.

Moving Averages and the Last Column

Unlike bar, candle and line charts, where the last bar changes every time frame and so the moving average value changes, the last column on a Point and Figure chart can take many time periods to build. One of three things can happen.

Firstly, the chart could remain unchanged, meaning that although the price is changing, it is not changing sufficiently to result in a lengthening of the column. In this case, the moving average value for the last column does not change. Secondly, the last column may lengthen as a price change results in a new box being plotted. In this case, the moving average value for the last column will change marginally because the midpoint of the last column has changed. Thirdly, the price may reverse sufficiently to result in a new column in the opposite direction. In this case, the proxy value for what was the last column is fixed, and so the moving average value for that column is fixed, and a new proxy value is calculated for the new last column in the opposite direction, resulting in a change in the moving average.

When moving averages were first used on Point and Figure charts, the moving average value for the last column was not plotted until the length of the column was fixed by a reversal. This meant that the moving average lagged the chart by one column. It is easy to understand that without a computer it was not possible to keep recalculating the moving average value as the last column lengthened, but that is no longer a restriction so moving averages are current.

WHAT ARE MOVING AVERAGES USED FOR?

Having understood how to construct and draw moving averages on Point and Figure charts, it is important to understand why they are used. The main purpose for using moving averages is to identify trend. The time horizon of the trend identified is determined by the length of the moving average. The greater the length, the longer the time horizon. Moving averages therefore are a substitute for drawing subjective and 45° trend lines.

By inspection, a rising moving average identifies a price uptrend and a falling moving average identifies a price downtrend, but of course it is not as easy as that. Once a trend is in place it is easy to see what the trend is by looking at the direction of the moving average, but knowing when the trend has changed from up to down or down to up is more difficult.

Technical analysts of time-based charts use a number of methods for determining when a price trend has changed. Besides observing the direction of the moving average, the position of the price in relation to the moving average determines the trend. If the price is above the moving average, the trend is up, if it is below, the trend is down, so the price crossing the moving average determines where the trend changes. Another method is to use two moving averages, and if the shorter length is above the longer length, the trend is up, and if it is below, the trend is down.

These methods are easy to use but are not without their problems, the main one being the occurrence of whipsaws, where the trend changes from up to down and down to up every few periods. This is an accepted hazard of using moving averages to determine trend and consequently generate buy and sell signals. The use of moving averages on Point and Figure charts goes some way to address this deficiency, but no method is perfect because sometimes prices trend up and down and sometimes they trend sideways, causing whipsaws.

HOW TO USE MOVING AVERAGES ON POINT AND FIGURE CHARTS

The time-based chart method of treating a price break above or below the moving average as a buy or sell signal is not possible with Point and Figure charts, because of the way moving averages are calculated. You will recall that moving averages on Point and Figure charts are not calculated on the last price in the column, but rather on the midpoint of each column, so the moving average does not follow the last X or last O in any column, rather it follows the midpoint of each column. Because columns of Xs and Os alternate, the last X and O in any column can oscillate through the moving average, crossing above and below the moving average nearly every time there is a column change.

You can see this in Chart 3-9, which is a Point and Figure chart with a 5 column moving average. Notice how the columns oscillate through the moving average making the fact that the latest X is above or the latest O is below the moving average unsuitable as a means of determining whether to buy or sell. This is the same whether the chart is a 3-box or 1-box reversal chart, therefore different methods of obtaining buy and sell signals from moving averages must be employed. Because the signals generated from 1-box and 3-box charts are different they are dealt with separately here, although the methods are in effect the same.

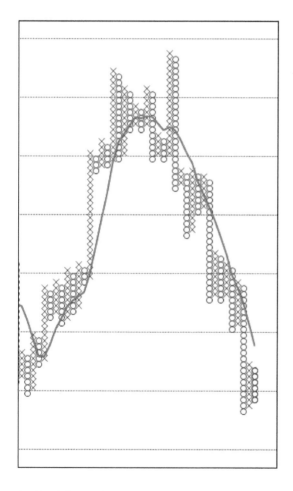

CHART 3-9: SHOWING THE PRICE CROSSING THE 5 COLUMN MOVING
AVERAGE ON NEARLY EVERY REVERSAL

What constitutes a cross of a moving average?

An X (or O) is deemed to have crossed above (or below) a moving average if the midpoint of the box has crossed above (or below) the moving average. This is easier to see with Xs as the midpoint of the box is the intersection of the diagonals, as shown in Figure 3-1. The midpoint of the left and right-hand Xs is above the red moving average. This means that a break above the blue horizontal line is a double-top buy above the moving average.

FIGURE 3-1: SHOWING THE MIDPOINT OF
THE X ABOVE THE MOVING AVERAGE

It is exactly the same consideration if columns of Os are breaking below the moving average.

Using Moving Averages on 3-Box Reversal Charts

When moving averages on 3-box reversal charts were discussed in *The Definitive Guide to Point and Figure*, only one method of using them was proposed. That method, which is method 1 below, entails using the position of the moving average to identify the trend, then waiting for the next Point and Figure signal to act. It was felt at the time that Point and Figure signals should overrule anything else. Further research has shown, however, that there are three ways to use moving averages on a 3-box reversal chart. The method you choose depends on the Point and Figure chart you are drawing.

The first method is to use the penetration of the moving average by an X or O as an alert, then to buy or sell on the next Point and Figure signal. The second method is to use the penetration of the moving average by the column midpoint as the signal to buy and sell, and the third method is to use the penetration of the moving average by the column midpoint as an alert, then to buy or sell on the next Point and Figure signal.

As explained earlier, it is not possible to use the simple cross of the moving average by the price as a signal – this could lead to a signal every column as columns cross up and down through the moving average.

Method 1 – Using the position of the moving average in conjunction with Point and Figure signals

The advantage of 3-box reversal charts is that double-top and double-bottom patterns are discrete and unambiguous. This means that they can be easily used to trigger buy and sell signals when used in conjunction with moving averages.

With this method, the position of the moving average is used to warn of a trend change and put you on alert to look for the next Point and Figure signal. So when an X breaks above the moving average, you are placed on buy alert to look for the next double-top buy, and when an O breaks below the moving average, you are placed on sell alert to look for the next double-bottom sell.

One of two things can happen when an X breaks above the moving average. If a double-top buy occurs, it is your signal to buy and all double-bottom sell signals are ignored while the price is above the moving average. If a double-top buy does not occur and a column of Os crosses below the moving average, your buy alert is cancelled and you are placed on a sell alert to look for the next double-bottom sell. This may mean you switch from buy alert to sell alert on each column change, but having to wait for the next Point and Figure signal prevents whipsaw signals.

Conversely, one of two things can happen when an O breaks below the moving average. If a double-bottom sell occurs, it is your signal to sell and all double-top buy signals are ignored while the price is below the moving average. If a double-bottom sell does not occur and a column of Xs crosses above the moving average, your sell alert is cancelled and you are placed on a buy alert to look for the next double-top buy.

Chart 3-10 shows a 3-box reversal chart with a 5 column moving average. The first buy signal occurs with a double-top buy at point A, which is made up of three columns as follows. First an X column crosses (just) above the moving average, placing you on buy alert, then an O column crosses below the moving average, cancelling the buy alert and placing you on sell alert. Next an X column crosses above the moving average again, placing you on buy alert again to take the next double-top buy. Because the X in the first column of the double-top is already above the moving average, the double-top buy occurs when the X column rises above the previous X column, shown by the horizontal blue line at point A.

Having bought at A, all additional double-top buys above the moving average are ignored, and although you are looking for sell signals, all double-bottom sell signals are ignored if they occur above the moving average. Note especially the double-bottom marked Z. This is not a sell signal because the first column of Os in the pattern did not penetrate the moving average and you are only placed on sell alert when the second column of Os in the pattern penetrates it. This means you would need to wait for another double-bottom sell, which does not occur. In other words, for it to be a valid double-bottom sell, the first O in the pattern must place you on alert and the second O must trigger the double-bottom sell, which was not the case at Z.

The next signal on the chart is a sell signal, which occurs with a double-bottom (actually a triple-bottom) sell at point B below the moving average. A sell alert occurs when the first column of Os in the pattern breaks below the moving average. Then, while the pattern is forming, you are placed on buy alert and sell alert a number of times as Xs and Os cross above and below the moving average. Finally, the third column of Os then breaks below the previous columns of Os, which is below the moving average shown by the horizontal line at point B, and the sell signal occurs.

Three columns later there is a strong rally, with a column of Xs rising above the moving average to point C. This puts you on buy alert to look for a double-top buy above the moving average, but no such signal occurs, so the sell at B remains in place. It is important to note that the double-top buy at point D occurred below the moving average and is therefore ignored. For a double-top to be valid, the midpoint of both Xs in the double top must be above the moving average. Conversely, for a sell to be valid, the midpoint of both Os must be below the moving average.

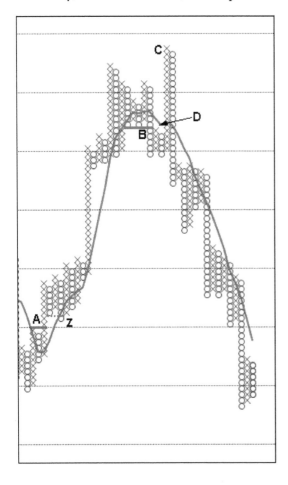

CHART 3-10: 3-BOX REVERSAL CHART SHOWING POINT AND FIGURE SIGNALS BASED ON THE POSITION OF THE 5 COLUMN MOVING AVERAGE

Using basic Point and Figure double-top and double-bottom signals with the moving average makes it very easy to see where the buys and sells occur and prevents whipsaws.

Method 2 – Using the position of the column midpoint and the moving average

With this method, the midpoint of the column crossing above or below the moving average is used to trigger buy and sell signals; buy when the midpoint crosses above the moving average and sell when it crosses below. No account is taken of Point and Figure signals themselves. As you have seen already, the midpoint of each column is the proxy for the column and the line that connects these proxy values is a 1 column moving average. So this method is therefore the crossing of any length moving average by the 1 column moving average.

Chart 3-11 shows the chart with a 1 column (red) moving average, which tracks the column midpoint, and a 20 column (blue) moving average. When the midpoint of the column, which is the 1 column moving average, crosses above the 20 column moving average it is a signal to buy, and when it crosses below it is a signal to sell. There is only one signal in this example, a sell signal, when the 1 column red average crosses below the blue 20 column average, circled.

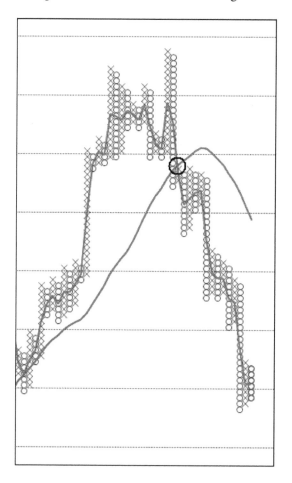

CHART 3-11: 3-BOX REVERSAL CHART SHOWING THE SIGNAL WHEN THE 1 COLUMN (RED) AVERAGE CROSSES BELOW THE 20 COLUMN (BLUE) AVERAGE

Since it is not possible in Chart 3-11 to see the exact position of the columns and moving averages at the time the midpoint crossed below the 20 column moving average, Chart 3-12 steps the chart back to the time of the crossover. Notice that the crossover did not occur during the long column of Os, which is what you would expect, because the midpoint of that column was well above the 20 column moving average. Instead it is the midpoint of the next X column that finally crosses below the 20 column moving average. This means that with this method, a sell signal can occur during a column of Xs, or a buy signal can occur during a column of Os.

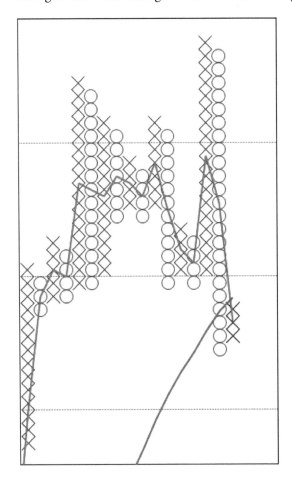

CHART 3-12: ENLARGED SECTION OF CHART 3-11 SHOWING EXACTLY
WHEN THE CIRCLED SIGNAL OCCURRED

Method 3 – Using the position of the column midpoint and the moving average in conjunction with Point and Figure signals

This method is a combination of methods 1 and 2, where the midpoint of the column crossing the moving average is used to place you on alert to take the next Point and Figure signal. So when the column midpoint (the 1 column moving average) breaks above the moving average, you are placed on buy alert to look for the next double-top buy. If a double-top buy does not occur and the column midpoint crosses below the moving average, your buy alert is cancelled and you are placed on a sell alert to look for the next double-bottom sell. Conversely, when the column midpoint breaks below the moving average, you are placed on sell alert to look for the next double-bottom sell. If a double-bottom sell does not occur and the column midpoint crosses above the moving average, your sell alert is cancelled and you are placed on a buy alert to look for the next double-top buy.

Chart 3-13 shows the same chart as Chart 3-11 and Chart 3-12, with a 1 column and 20 column moving average. Once again there is only one signal – a sell signal at point A, when a double-bottom sell occurs whilst the 1 column average is below the 20 column average.

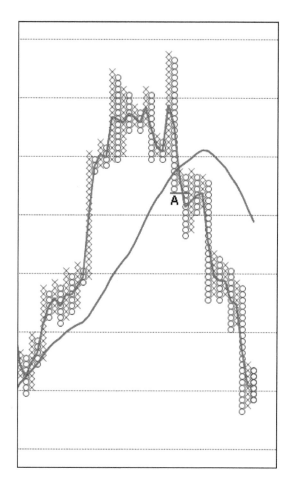

CHART 3-13: 3-BOX REVERSAL CHART SHOWING A POINT AND FIGURE SELL SIGNAL
AFTER THE 1 COLUMN AVERAGE HAS CROSSED THE 20 COLUMN AVERAGE

Using Moving Averages on 1-Box Reversal Charts

When the use of moving averages on 1-box charts was discussed in *The Definitive Guide to Point and Figure* it was felt that only complete semi-catapult or fulcrum patterns in conjunction with the position of the moving average could be used to generate buy and sell signals. It is now felt that this is too restrictive, so consideration is now given to simple X or O column breakouts instead of complete patterns. This makes the analysis of 1-box charts less subjective. One of the difficulties with 1-box charts is that the equivalent of a 3-box double-top and double-bottom has many variations.

Figure 3-2 shows a small sample of possible 1-box X column breakouts. Pattern A looks just like a 3-box double-top with a column of Os, albeit with only two Os between the two X columns. Patterns B to E are typical 1-box semi-catapult patterns where the current column of Xs has broken above the previous X. Pattern F is an example of a one-step-back during an uptrend. Finally pattern G is slightly different from the other patterns. It looks like a one-step back but it is not, although it is still a column of Xs rising above an X in the previous column.

Although the patterns can evolve in different ways, a buy signal is still essentially a column of Xs rising above a previous X. It could be the previous column as in patterns B, D, E, F and G, or it could be separated by an O column as shown in patterns A and C. A sell signal is a column of Os falling below a previous O. With 3-box charts, there is always a column of Os between the two columns of Xs or a column of Xs between two columns of Os. With a 1-box chart, however, that may not be the case – as you can see in Figure 3-2.

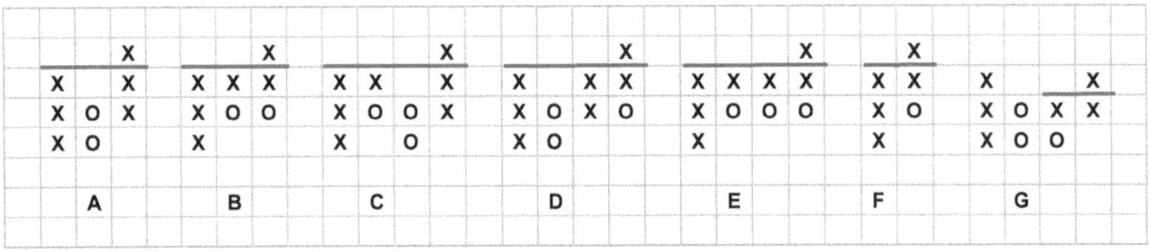

```
        X               X               X               X                   X           X
  X     X         X X X         X X         X         X X         X X X X         X X         X             X
  X O X         X O O         X O O X         X O X O         X O O O         X O         X O X X
  X O             X             X     O         X O             X             X             X O O

        A               B               C               D                   E           F             G
```

FIGURE 3-2: SHOWING 1-BOX SEMI-CATAPULT BUY SIGNALS

Although it is more difficult to spot Point and Figure signals on 1-box charts, all three methods used for 3-box charts can be used with 1-box charts. You should note, however, that although it is common practice to draw 1-box charts as 'point' charts using Xs only, you will need to draw 1-box charts with moving averages as XO Point and Figure charts otherwise you will have difficulty seeing the Xs breaking above Xs and Os breaking below Os clearly.

Method 1 – Using the position of the moving average in conjunction with Point and Figure signals

With this method, when a column of Xs rises above the moving average you are placed on buy alert. You then buy when a new X breaks above an X in a previous column, provided both Xs are above the moving average. The first X may be one or more columns away from the breakout X. If the break above does not occur, and an O falls below the moving average, your buy alert is cancelled and you are placed on sell alert. You then sell when an O breaks below an O in a previous column, provided both Os are below the moving average. In a similar way to 3-box charts, it is possible to swing from buy alert to sell alert without either signal occurring.

Chart 3-14 is a 1-box reversal chart with a 5 column moving average showing a similar section of data to the 3-box chart in Chart 3-10. The first buy signal occurs at point A, with a typical double-top buy, which is the first Point and Figure signal after an X has risen above the moving average. As with 3-box charts, once you have acted on a buy signal, you ignore any new buy and sell signals that occur above the moving average. You are looking for a double-bottom sell which occurs below the moving average. The next signal is a one-step back sell signal, which occurs below the moving average at point B. One column later the price rises above the moving average to place you on buy alert with a buy signal coming with the double-top buy at point C. The price then falls below the moving average, with the sell signal coming at point D, which is a triple-bottom sell. The price then rises above the moving average again with a one-step back buy signal coming at point E. Finally, the price falls below the moving average with the double-bottom sell signal coming at point F.

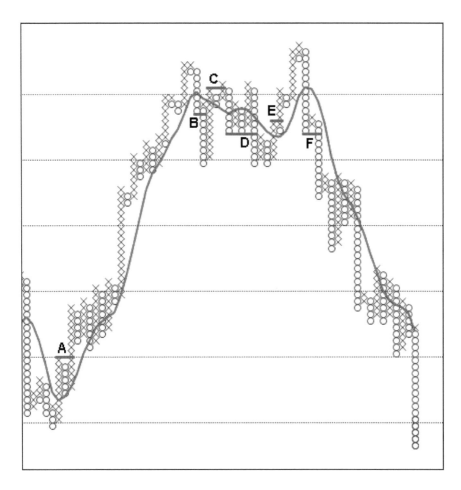

CHART 3-14: 1-BOX REVERSAL CHART SHOWING POINT AND FIGURE SIGNALS BASED ON THE POSITION OF THE 5 COLUMN MOVING AVERAGE

You can see that there have been a number of whipsaws between signals B and F. This is because 1-box charts have wider patterns. As Point and Figure charts widen, so the length of the moving average needs to be increased. Increasing the moving average to 25 columns, for example, removes the signals between A and F, as shown in Chart 3-15.

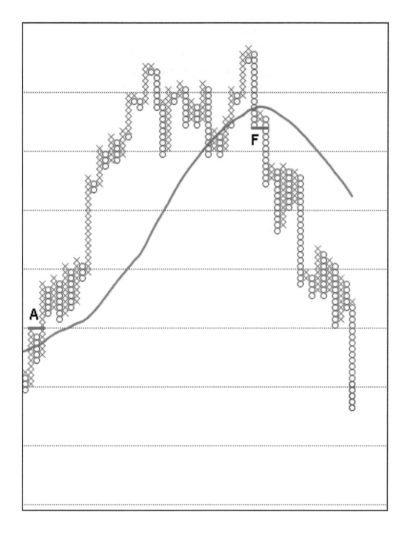

CHART 3-15: 1-BOX REVERSAL CHART SHOWING POINT AND FIGURE SIGNALS BASED ON THE POSITION OF THE 25 COLUMN MOVING AVERAGE

Method 2 – Using the position of the column midpoint and the moving average

As with 3-box reversal charts, this method relies on the midpoint of the column crossing above or below the moving average to trigger buy and sell signals; buy when the midpoint crosses above the moving average and sell when it crosses below. Once again, the midpoint of each column is measured by the 1 column moving average, so this method is the crossing of the chosen moving average by the 1 column moving average.

Chart 3-16 is a 1-box chart with a 1 column moving average (red), which tracks the column midpoint, and a 20 column moving average (blue). Buys are generated at points A and C when the midpoint of the column represented by the 1 column moving average crosses above the 20 column moving average. Sells are generated at points B and D when the 1 column average crosses below the 20 column average. No regard is taken of any Point and Figure signals.

As with 3-box charts, the penetration of the 20 column average by the 1 column average may occur in the next column and not the column that it appears to have occurred in the completed chart. For example, the sell signal at point D occurred in the next X column and not the O column.

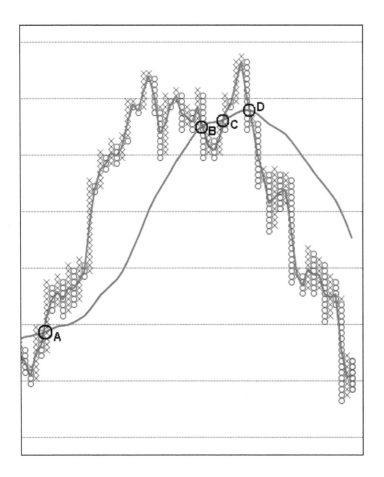

CHART 3-16: 1-BOX REVERSAL CHART SHOWING SIGNALS GENERATED BY 1 COLUMN (RED) CROSSING 20 COLUMN (BLUE) MOVING AVERAGE

Method 3 – Using the position of the column midpoint and the moving average in conjunction with Point and Figure signals

Once again this method is a combination of methods 1 and 2, where the midpoint of the column crossing the moving average is used to place you on alert to take the next Point and Figure signal. Remember, with 1-box charts a buy occurs when an X breaks above an X in a previous column, provided both Xs are above the moving average; a sell occurs when an O breaks below an O in a previous column, provided both Os are below the moving average. In either case, the *previous column* may be one or more columns away from the latest column.

So, when the column midpoint breaks above the moving average you are placed on buy alert to look for the next Point and Figure buy signal. If a buy does not occur and the column midpoint crosses below the moving average, your buy alert is cancelled and you are placed on a sell alert to look for the next sell.

Conversely, when the column midpoint breaks below the moving average you are placed on sell alert to look for the next double-bottom sell. If a double-bottom sell does not occur and the column midpoint crosses above the moving average, your sell alert is cancelled and you are placed on a buy alert to look for the next double-top buy.

Chart 3-17 is the same chart as Chart 3-15 and Chart 3-16, with a 1 column and 20 column average. The 1 column moving average crosses above the 20 column moving average placing you on buy alert, then a double-top buy occurs at point A. When it crosses below you are placed on sell alert and must wait for the next Point and Figure sell signal, which occurs at point B.

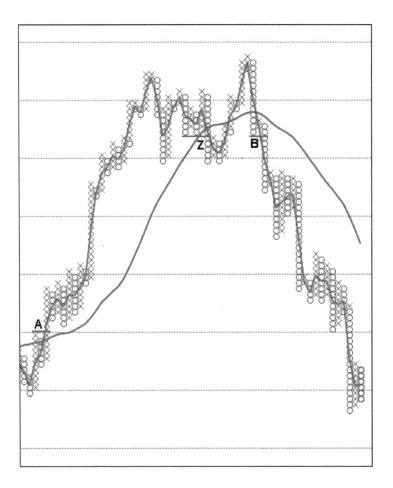

CHART 3-17: 1-BOX REVERSAL CHART SHOWING A POINT AND FIGURE SIGNAL AFTER 1 COLUMN HAS CROSSED THE 20 COLUMN AVERAGE

If you are wondering why there was no sell signal with the triple-bottom sell at point Z, take a look at Chart 3-18, which shows that section of the chart enlarged. You can see that you were not placed on sell alert because the 1 column average had not crossed below the 20 column average when the triple-bottom occurred.

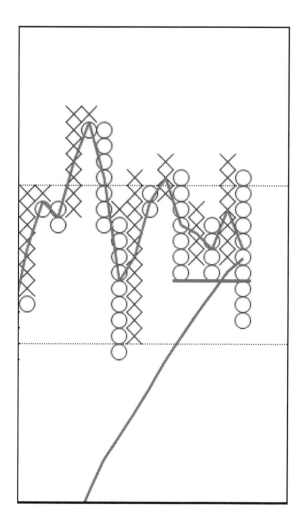

CHART 3-18: THE SECTION MARKED Z IN CHART 3-17 ENLARGED TO SHOW WHY NO SIGNAL OCCURRED

Using Two Moving Averages on Point and Figure

With bar, line and candlestick analysis, it is customary to use two moving averages to obtain signals. Methods 2 and 3, where the midpoint crosses the moving average, are the same as using two moving averages. This is because a line joining the midpoint of each column is equivalent to a 1 column moving average. The strategy with two moving averages of any length is the same; buy when the shorter average crosses above the longer and sell when it crosses below. You may add the additional filter of waiting for the next Point and Figure signal.

As you have seen in Method 3 – when the 1 column average was used to mark out the midpoint of each column – you need to be careful when looking at a completed chart because what may appear to be a signal was not in fact a signal at the time the column was being built.

Long/Short

In discussing all three methods with 3-box and 1-box above, consideration was only given to trading long, but these methods may also be used to trade short, as well as adding to existing positions. For example, methods 1 and 3 ignore any new Point and Figure signals after the initial one. However, it is possible to use subsequent double-top buy signals above the moving average as a signal to add to an existing position, and double-bottom sell signals above the moving average to take profits. It is also possible to use double-bottom sell signals below the moving average to sell short and to add to shorts, or double-top buy signals below the moving average to take profits on short positions.

Using Moving Averages on Other Box Reversal Charts

The use of moving averages on other box reversal charts such as 2-box or 5-box is exactly the same as that for 3-box reversal charts, which was covered on page 48.

Choosing Moving Average Lengths

The choice of moving average length is a problem for any technical analyst. This is less of an issue if methods 1 and 3 are used because there are a finite number of Point and Figure buy and sell signals. This means that small adjustments to the moving average length make little difference to when the signals are generated.

Using the midpoint of each column as the proxy value for the column has the effect of smoothing the data on which Point and Figure moving averages are calculated. You can see this by referring to Chart 3-1 and Chart 3-2, showing the line connecting the midpoint of each column. Because the data is already smoothed, there is no need to use longer length moving averages to smooth it further.

Close, High/Low, Low/High or OHLC Construction

It has already been intimated that the construction of the Point and Figure chart makes a big difference to the moving averages used, because the moving average is calculated from the chart and not the raw data. High/low, low/high and ohlc construction all produce different and wider patterns with shorter length columns than close only. For this reason, moving average lengths will have to be increased on charts constructed using these methods in order to avoid whipsaws.

Moving Average Calculations

There are many ways to calculate a moving average, the most common being simple[12] and exponential.[13] The simple method allocates equal weights to all the prices in the average, while the exponential method weights the prices exponentially, allocating the greatest weight to the latest prices. Because of this, the exponential turns quicker than the simple because the last column has more effect on the average. It is not the purpose of this book to go into any depth regarding moving average calculations except to say that any calculation is possible with Point and Figure charts.

MOVING AVERAGE CHART EXAMPLES

3-box reversal

Chart 3-19 is a 1% x 3 of gold with 45° trend lines so you can see where the price crossed trend lines. Chart 3-20 is the same gold chart with a 20 column moving average with blue and red arrows showing where the Point and Figure buy and sell signals occurred. This is using method 1, the position of the moving average as the alert and the next double-top or double-bottom as the signal.

CHART 3-19: 1% X 3 OF GOLD WITH 45° TREND LINES

---

12 Simple average St = (Pt + Pt-1 +....Pt-(n-1))/n
13 Exponential average Et = f *Pt + (1-f) * Et-1

You can see immediately that the signals generated by the moving average occur earlier in Chart 3-20 than in Chart 3-19, but that there are a number of whipsaws.

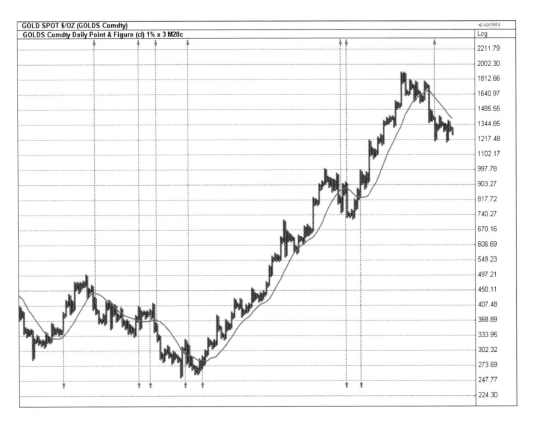

CHART 3-20: 1% X 3 OF GOLD WITH 20 COLUMN MOVING AVERAGE SHOWING SIGNALS BASED ON POINT AND FIGURE SIGNALS USING METHOD 1

Chart 3-21 is the gold chart again with a 1 column and 20 column moving average. This is method 3, using the position of column midpoint and the moving average as the alert and the next double-top or double-bottom as the signal. The blue and red arrows show the positions of those double-top and double bottom signals. You can see that in this case, method 3 delivers the best signals with fewer whipsaws. This doesn't mean method 3 will always be the best, however.

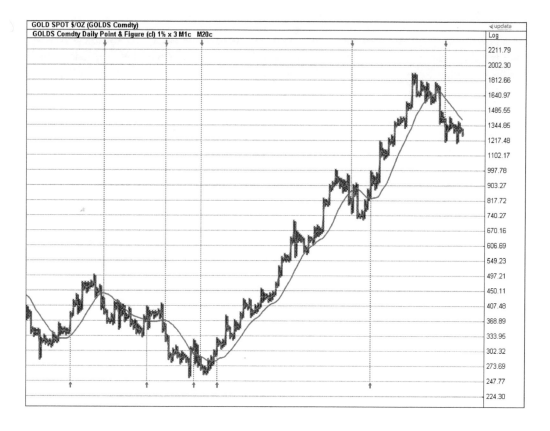

CHART 3-21: 1% X 3 OF GOLD WITH 20 COLUMN MOVING AVERAGE SHOWING SIGNALS BASED ON THE MIDPOINT CROSSING THE MOVING AVERAGE AND POINT AND FIGURE SIGNALS USING METHOD 3

Adding moving average bands

It is possible to eliminate more false signals and improve on method 3 by adding percentage bands either side of the moving average. In Chart 3-22, 5% bands have been added to the 20 column moving average. This means the X or O columns must move 5% above or below the moving average before you are alerted to take the next double-top or double-bottom signal.

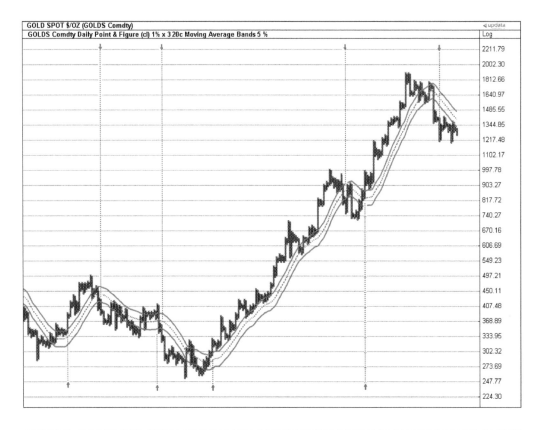

CHART 3-22: 1% X 3 OF GOLD WITH 20 COLUMN MOVING AVERAGE WITH 5% BANDS SHOWING SIGNALS BASED ON POINT AND FIGURE SIGNALS OUTSIDE THE BANDS

1-box reversal

It is not really possible to compare moving averages with trend lines on 1-box charts because the subjective placement of trend lines with hindsight will always be superior to any moving average crossover method.

Chart 3-23 is a 1% x 1 of the NASDAQ 100 with a 20 column moving average. The blue and red arrows show the buy signals and sell signals using method 1. Chart 3-24 is the same chart showing buy and sell signals using method 3 and Chart 3-25 is the chart showing Point and Figure signals above and below 5% moving average bands.

Notice that there is no difference in the signals between method 1 and 3, but there is a significant improvement when a 5% filter is placed above and below the moving average. You will also see an improvement in methods 1 and 3 if you increase the length of the moving average. Chart 3-26 is the same chart with a 30 column moving average, showing improved signals using method 3.

CHART 3-23: 1% X 1 OF THE NASDAQ 100 WITH 20 COLUMN MOVING AVERAGE SHOWING SIGNALS BASED ON POINT AND FIGURE SIGNALS, METHOD 1

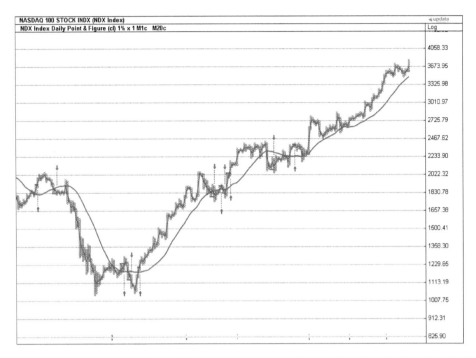

CHART 3-24: 1% X 1 OF THE NASDAQ 100 WITH 20 COLUMN MOVING AVERAGE SHOWING SIGNALS BASED ON THE MIDPOINT OF THE COLUMN AND POINT AND FIGURE SIGNALS, METHOD 3

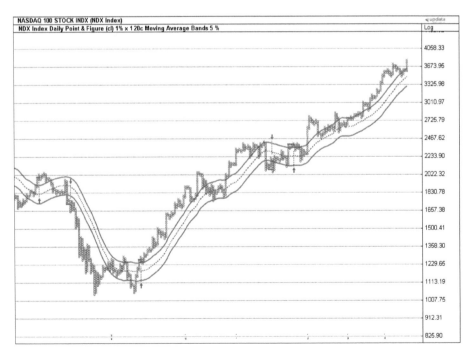

CHART 3-25: 1% X 1 OF THE NASDAQ 100 WITH 20 COLUMN MOVING AVERAGE AND 5% BANDS SHOWING SIGNALS OUTSIDE THE BANDS

CHART 3-26: 1% X 1 OF THE NASDAQ 100 WITH 30 COLUMN MOVING AVERAGE SHOWING SIGNALS BASED ON THE MIDPOINT OF THE COLUMN AND POINT AND FIGURE SIGNALS, METHOD 3

THE 4TH METHOD

In addition to the three methods for using moving averages with Point and Figure discussed above, there is a 4th method which you may wish to consider. It is the method used with Donchian channels and Bollinger bands in the next chapter. Methods 1 and 3 above use the position of the moving average as the alert to take the next Point and Figure signal. Method 4 is slightly different in that it does not have to be a traditional Point and Figure signal, but rather just a break above or below the alerting column whenever that occurs. In many cases, this is also a Point and Figure signal, but in some cases it is not. The alerting column is the first column to break through the moving average. Below are various examples of what can happen and how the signals differ.

In Figure 3-3 the first column of Os to break below the moving average is the alerting column. A line is then drawn across the low of the break column, marked A. With method 4, a break below this line is the signal to sell. This is an example where using method 4 waiting for a break below the alerting column, marked A, avoids a false sell signal from the double-bottom using method 1, marked B.

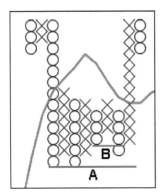

FIGURE 3-3: SHOWING THE CASE WHERE USING METHOD 4 AVOIDS A
FALSE SELL SIGNAL (AT B) THAT WOULD HAVE BEEN GIVEN BY METHOD 1

Figure 3-4 shows the case where the signal from method 4, marked A, occurs earlier than the double-bottom sell signal from method 1, marked B.

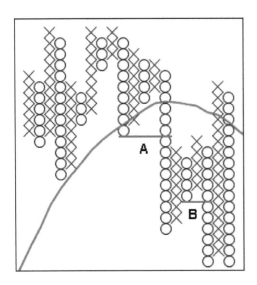

FIGURE 3-4: SHOWING THE CASE WHERE USING METHOD 4
PRODUCES AN EARLIER SIGNAL THAN METHOD 1

Figure 3-5 shows the case where the signal from method 4 and method 1 occur at the same time, so the signal from method 4 is also a Point and Figure signal.

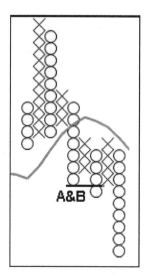

FIGURE 3-5: SHOWING THE CASE WHERE THE SIGNAL FROM METHOD 4 AND
METHOD 1 ARE SIMULTANEOUS AS BOTH ARE A POINT AND FIGURE SIGNAL

As you can see, there are cases where method 4 is superior to method 1 and some where it is not. If you look at the chart examples above and at your own charts, you will seldom see an occasion where method 4 is different from method 1 because the signals tend to occur at the same time. However, method 4 is detailed here for your consideration. More information can be found in Chapter 4, which covers the use of this method with Donchian channels and Bollinger bands.

SUMMARY

Although not a 21st century technique, moving averages on Point and Figure charts were resurrected in the late 20th century to become the favoured technique of the 21st century. The ability to draw moving averages on their charts has provided Point and Figure analysts with another tool with which to identify trend, where in the past they had been restricted to the use of trend lines.

The length of a moving average on Point and Figure charts is based on the number of columns and the proxy for each column used to calculate the moving average is the midpoint of each column. These are moving averages of the Point and Figure chart, not of the raw underlying data. For this reason, changes in the Point and Figure parameters change the Point and Figure chart and hence the path of the moving average, even though the length remains unchanged. This means that you should decide your Point and Figure parameters first, then apply moving averages to identify the trend.

A number of methods for using moving averages on Point and Figure charts have been presented, some of which incorporate Point and Figure signals into the moving average crossover. You will have seen that the wider the chart patterns become, the longer the moving average length needs to be, so 1-box charts tend to require moving averages of greater length. Moving average bands can also be used to filter out a number of false signals.

Chapter Four. Using Other Tools on Point and Figure Charts

INTRODUCTION

I N ADDITION TO MOVING AVERAGES AND MOVING AVERAGE BANDS covered in the previous chapter, other calculated lines may be drawn and used on Point and Figure charts. In this chapter the use of Donchian channels, Bollinger bands and Parabolic SAR is explained. Although some of these were introduced in *The Definitive Guide to Point and Figure*, they are very much 21st century techniques and therefore they are included here.

Bollinger bands stem from the moving average calculation already covered in the previous chapter, Parabolic SAR is not related to moving averages at all, but acts in a similar way, and Donchian channels mark the chart with automatic levels based on column highs and lows.

DONCHIAN CHANNELS

Donchian channels were developed by a market technician named Richard Donchian. They are made up of two lines, one plotting the highest high and the other plotting the lowest low over a defined number of periods. In Point and Figure terms, it is a defined number of columns over which they are plotted. Donchian channels are ideally suited to Point and Figure charts because, by plotting lines across the highest X and lowest O over a selected number of columns, they can be used to provide levels at which a change in trend is signalled.

Since they are drawn from the highest high and lowest low of the columns under consideration, by definition the price can never break out of the channels, so in order to allow a price break, a number of columns must be omitted before the look back. Although omitting 1 column is enough to achieve a breakout, around 5 is more common. However, changing the number of columns which are ignored has the effect of shifting the channels to the right and therefore changes the column on which the breakout occurs; the fewer the columns that are ignored, the earlier the breakout. Chart 4-1 is a 1% x 3 of the S&P 500 with three 20 column Donchian channels, the red ignoring the last 1 column, the blue ignoring the last 5 columns and black ignoring the last 20 columns. The circled section in Chart 4-1 is shown in detail in Chart 4-2.

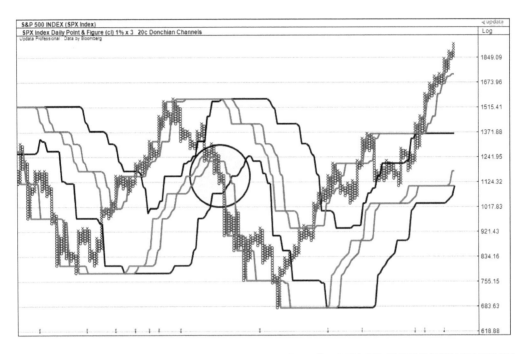

CHART 4-1: 1% X 3 OF THE S&P 500 WITH THREE 20 COLUMN DONCHIAN CHANNELS, RED IGNORING THE LAST 1 COLUMN, BLUE IGNORING THE LAST 5 COLUMNS AND BLACK IGNORING THE LAST 20 COLUMNS

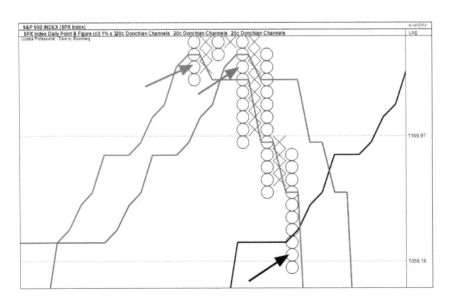

CHART 4-2: CIRCLED SECTION IN CHART 4-1 ENLARGED, SHOWING THE DIFFERENT BREAKOUT COLUMNS WHEN 1, 5 AND 20 COLUMNS ARE IGNORED

The enlarged section in Chart 4-2 shows a red arrow pointing to the O column that breaks below the red (ignoring 1 column) channel, a blue arrow showing the O column that breaks below the blue (ignoring 5 columns) channel and a black arrow showing the O column that breaks below the black (ignoring 20 columns) channel. This allows you to see the different signals produced when altering the number of columns ignored.

Changing the number of columns in the look back affects the number of columns that are ignored. It also has an effect on the signals produced. Reducing the number of columns in the look back narrows the channel and therefore changes the column on which the breakout occurs; the shorter the look back, the closer the two channels are to one another and the shorter the time horizon.

Chart 4-3 is the same chart as Chart 4-1, but with red 20 column look back and blue 10 column look back Donchian channels, both ignoring the last 5 columns. The circled section in Chart 4-3 is shown in detail in Chart 4-4.

The enlarged section in Chart 4-4 shows a red arrow pointing to the O column that breaks below the red 20 column channel and a blue arrow pointing to the O column that breaks below the blue 10 column channel. This shows that the shorter the look back, the earlier the channels are penetrated.

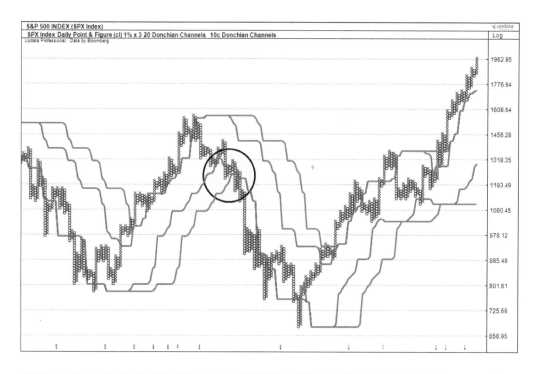

CHART 4-3: 1% X 3 OF THE S&P 500 WITH A RED 20 COLUMN DONCHIAN CHANNEL AND A BLUE 10 COLUMN DONCHIAN CHANNEL, BOTH IGNORING THE LAST 5 COLUMNS

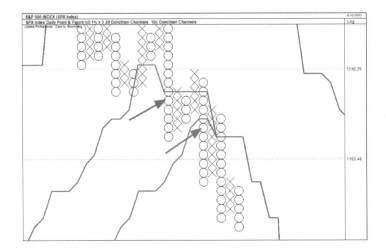

CHART 4-4: CIRCLED SECTION IN CHART 4-3 ENLARGED, SHOWING THE DIFFERENT BREAKOUT COLUMNS WITH DIFFERENT LOOK BACK DONCHIAN CHANNELS

On Point and Figure charts, Donchian channels are a good substitute for 45° trend lines and moving averages. They are, in effect, trend following support and resistance lines. The channel direction defines the trend and the breaks of the channel in the opposite direction define the turning points. Notice how the price hugs and sometimes exceeds the upper channel in uptrends and likewise hugs and sometimes exceeds the lower channel in downtrends.

Donchian channels also work with 1-box reversal charts and are therefore an objective way to define trends, which is something that is difficult on 1-box charts. Using the S&P 500 again for comparison with the charts above, Chart 4-5 is a 1-box reversal chart. Notice how the channels define the trend and define where the support and resistance levels are, making the trend analysis of the chart less subjective.

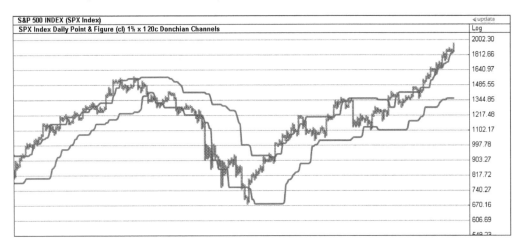

CHART 4-5: 1% X 1 OF THE S&P 500 WITH A 20 COLUMN DONCHIAN CHANNEL IGNORING 5 COLUMNS

Obtaining buy and sell signals using Donchian channels

In addition to defining trend and providing support and resistance levels, Donchian channels can be used to generate buy and sell signals. The way signals are obtained is slightly different from those obtained from moving averages although the method, described as the 4th method, was explained on page 69.

Whereas with moving averages a cross of the moving average places you on alert to look for the next Point and Figure double-top or double-bottom signal, with Donchian channels the break out of the channel places you on alert to act if the level marked by the break is exceeded. So the high of the X column break above the upper channel becomes the column high marker, which if exceeded, becomes the signal to buy. The low of the O column break below the lower channel becomes the column low marker, which if exceeded, becomes the signal to sell.

Although many of these breaks above or below the markers may actually be Point and Figure double-top or double-bottom signals, they don't have to be. The reason for the difference in analysis is that, unlike moving averages and moving average bands, Donchian channels are not based on the midpoint of each column and so don't follow every turn in the price. Therefore after a break above the upper channel, the price can retrace back between the channels without affecting the direction of the channels themselves. What can happen then, for example, is that the upper channel can continue to be penetrated by one X, but the price retracement may mean that double-tops never occur outside the channels. For this reason, it is the penetration of the column high and low markers, no matter how many columns there are between the marker and the penetration column, that is the signal.

Taking the S&P 500 again, Chart 4-6 shows the markers placed at the tops of X column breakouts above the channels and at the bottom of the O column breakouts below the channels. Buy and sell signals are generated when the price breaks above or below these markers.

At point A, when a column of Xs breaks above the upper Donchian channel, a blue marker is drawn across the top of the breakout column. Four columns later an X breaks above the blue high marker and a buy is signalled. In this case it is a triple-top pattern (actually, it is a good example of a catapult), but it does not have to be – the signal is simply a break above the marker. The price remains in an uptrend until point B, when a column of Os breaks below the lower channel for the first time and a blue marker is drawn across the low of the breakout column of Os. Despite the price rallying back into the channels, four columns later an O breaks below the low marker and a sell is signalled at point B. You may notice that 5 columns to the left of point B, at point Z, an O can be seen to be partially below the lower band. It would be up to you whether you decide if this is a break or not.

At point C another buy is signalled in a similar fashion, but notice what happens at point D. A column of Os breaks below the lower channel and a marker is drawn, but at no stage does the price break below the marker so no sell is signalled and the buy at point C remains in place.

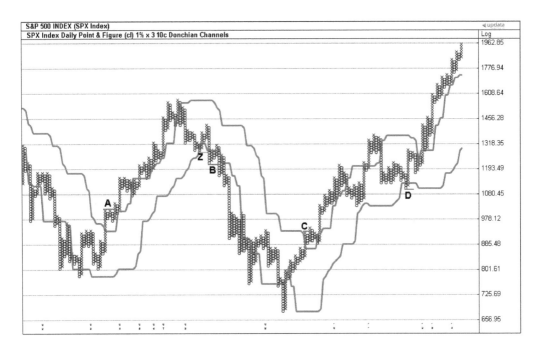

CHART 4-6: 1% X 3 OF THE S&P 500 WITH A 20 COLUMN DONCHIAN CHANNEL IGNORING 5 COLUMNS AND SHOWING SIGNALS

The same method can be employed with 1-box reversal charts. Chart 4-7 is a 1-box reversal chart of the S&P 500 showing similar buy and sells signals to the 3-box reversal chart above. Buy signals are marked A and C, the sell signal is marked B, and once again at point D there is a low marker that was not breached.

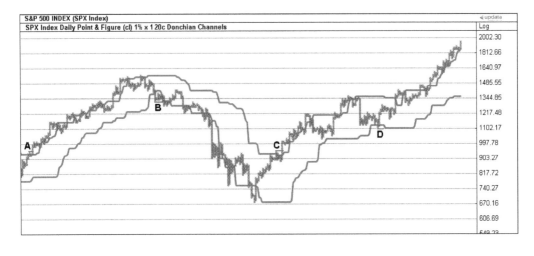

CHART 4-7: 1% X 1 OF THE S&P 500 WITH A 20 COLUMN DONCHIAN CHANNEL IGNORING 5 COLUMNS AND SHOWING SIGNALS

Donchian channels work in the same way with intraday data. Chart 4-8 is a 1 minute chart of Google Inc, with 5 column Donchian channels. 5 column is used instead of 10 or 20 because the chart is very short term. Once again, the buy and sell signals are marked in the same way; buys at points A, C and E, sells at points B and D. The break below the lower channel at point Z is marked as an alert, but the price never breaks below that level so no sell is recorded.

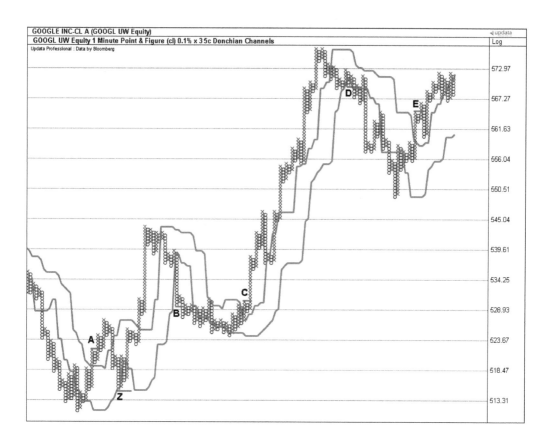

CHART 4-8: MINUTE 0.01% X 3 OF GOOGLE INC WITH 5 COLUMN DONCHIAN CHANNEL SHOWING SIGNALS

Donchian channels are extremely effective on Point and Figure charts because of the way Point and Figure charts compartmentalise prices into boxes. The channels based on highs and lows over a defined number of columns provide a guide to the trend and provide levels out of which breakouts become important. You have seen that a simple set of rules provides objective signals.

BOLLINGER BANDS

Bollinger bands were devised by John Bollinger and are one of the most popular tools used by technical analysts on candle, bar and line charts. They are volatility bands drawn a specified number of standard deviations, usually 2, above and below a moving average. The use of these on Point and Figure charts was never thought possible until it was discovered that moving averages could be drawn on non-time-based charts. Bollinger suggests a length of 20 periods with time-based charts, but you will find that 10 columns works well with Point and Figure charts.

The reason for using Bollinger bands is that they provide additional information about the chart and the state it is in. Adding the bands allows you to see areas where the trend is strong and where a trend change is coming. They show areas of low volatility, which always precede a breakout, although the direction of the breakout is not part of Bollinger bands analysis. Bollinger himself states that Bollinger bands do not give buy and sell signals based on the price touching the bands, but it is possible to use them to help in generating signals with Point and Figure charts in the same way in which Donchian channels are used above.

Obtaining buy and sell signals using Bollinger bands

Chart 4-9 is a 1% x 3 of the S&P 500 with 10 column, 2 standard deviation Bollinger bands. Notice that the strength of the trend is demonstrated by the price hugging the upper and lower bands. However, unlike Donchian channels described earlier, with Bollinger bands most of the price action is contained inside the bands. With 10 column bands it is usual that the Xs and Os penetrate the upper and lower bands when the trend is strong. The first warning that the trend is changing is when, after an uptrend, an O column penetrates the lower band, or when, after a downtrend, an X column penetrates the upper band. A penetration of the band is the alert, and places a marker, which if broken generates a signal.

At point A an X breaks the upper band and a marker, a blue resistance level, is drawn across the top of the X. Once an X breaks above the marker, a buy is generated. In this case it is a triple-top (actually, it is a catapult), but the pattern itself is not important, it is the fact that it has broken above the marker that is significant. The X breaking above the marker does not need to be outside the upper band.

The first alert to a sell occurs at point B and a marker is placed below the first O that breaks below the lower band. Four columns later the support created by the marker is broken and a sell signal is generated. Notice that the pattern is not a typical Point and Figure pattern, although some may have called it an extended double or triple bottom. Notice that 5 columns later the price rallied up to the upper band but because the X did not penetrate the band it was not marked. Even if it had been marked, it would not have been broken anyway.

The next breach of the upper band occurs at C and two columns later the level is broken, generating a buy. The lower band is penetrated at D and E and a marker is placed; however, in neither case was the support provided by the marker breached so no sell was generated and the buy at C remains in place. Note that markers remain valid until the band on the opposite side is breached. If you compare Chart 4-9 with Chart 4-6 you will see the signals, although not identical, are similar.

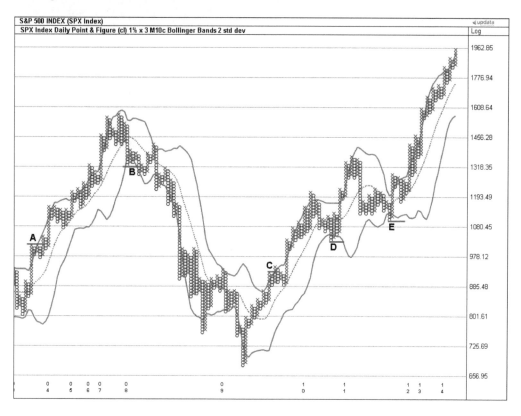

CHART 4-9: 1% X 3 OF S&P 500 WITH 10 COLUMN, 2 STANDARD DEVIATION BOLLINGER BANDS SHOWING SIGNALS

Bollinger band squeeze

Besides showing trend strength and generating trend change signals, Bollinger bands also show up low volatility areas which usually precede a sharp move. Called the 'squeeze', these occur when the bands converge like they did in the area marked E in Chart 4-9. The squeeze only tells you that there is about to be a sharp move – it does not tell you the direction.

The squeeze shows up better on charts with wider patterns, so those constructed with high/low or low/high data and 1-box reversal charts. Chart 4-10 is a 3-box reversal low/high constructed chart of the S&P with two clear squeezes circled. Because the chart is log scaled, you can count the number of boxes between the bands in the squeeze and compare it to other squeezes. In Chart 4-10, each box is 1% so the 5 boxes in the squeeze amount to a 5% difference between the bands.

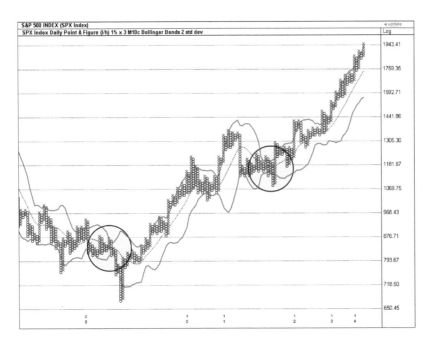

CHART 4-10: 1% X 3 LOW/HIGH CHART OF S&P 500 WITH 10 COLUMN, 2 STANDARD DEVIATION BOLLINGER BANDS SHOWING SQUEEZES

Chart 4-11 is a 1-box reversal low/high constructed chart showing more squeezes circled.

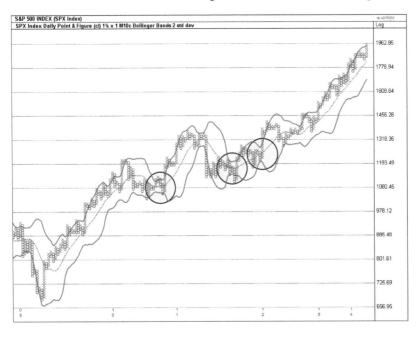

CHART 4-11: 1% X 1 LOW/HIGH CHART OF S&P 500 WITH 10 COLUMN, 2 STANDARD DEVIATION BOLLINGER BANDS SHOWING SQUEEZES

Squeezes also show up on intraday interval charts. Chart 4-12 is an hourly 3-box reversal low/high constructed chart with the squeezes circled.

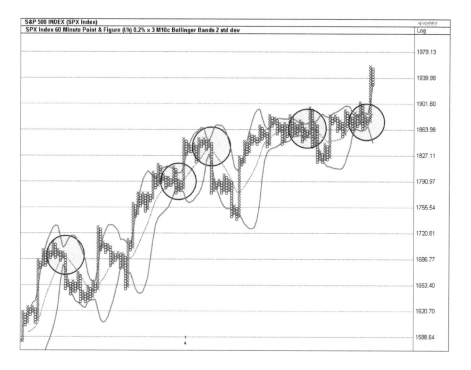

CHART 4-12: HOURLY 0.2% X 3 LOW/HIGH CHART OF S&P 500 WITH 10 COLUMN, 2 STANDARD DEVIATION BOLLINGER BANDS SHOWING SQUEEZES

Bollinger bands are a powerful tool. In Point and Figure form you have seen that they help to generate unambiguous buy and sell signals from the bands, which is difficult to do with Bollinger bands on time-based charts. Even without the signals, the bands enhance the Point and Figure chart, showing up areas of strong trend and areas of low volatility which occur before sharp moves.

PARABOLIC STOP AND REVERSE (SAR)

The Parabolic SAR was devised by J. Welles Wilder and presented in his 1978 book *New Concepts in Technical Trading Techniques.* Although it is a series of dots drawn on a Point and Figure chart, it does not use any of the logic used for calculating and drawing moving averages or Bollinger bands. Nevertheless, the way it is used is very similar to the way moving averages are used.

The calculation for the Parabolic may be found in Wilder's book and is therefore not detailed here. The only difference is that with bar and candle charts it uses the high and low of each bar or time period, whereas with Point and Figure charts it uses the high and low of each column instead. Because the SAR in Parabolic SAR means 'stop and reverse', the Parabolic is designed to keep you in the market all the time, either long or short, which fits well with Point and Figure charts, where the chart is either bullish or bearish based on the last signal.

Parabolic stops, unlike simple fixed percentage trailing stops, have an acceleration factor which allows them to start some distance away from the price after the initial signal, but accelerate towards the price as the trend matures, which is an ideal way to use trailing stops. The Parabolic calculation automatically tightens your stop as the trend matures. This can be seen in Chart 4-13, which is a 1% x 3 chart of the Dow Jones Industrial Average with a 0.02 Parabolic. When a column of Os breaches[14] the bullish (blue) Parabolic, the Parabolic line switches to the other side of the price, becoming the bearish (red) Parabolic. It starts a calculated distance away from the price, then as the downtrend matures it moves closer to the price action until it is breached by a column of Xs. When that happens, the Parabolic switches back to bullish (blue), again starting a calculated distance away from the price.

The circled section in Chart 4-13 is shown in detail in Charts 4-14 and 4-15. Chart 4-14 shows the position of the parabolic marked with the blue arrow, just before the column of Os penetrates it. At this stage the parabolic is still bullish. Chart 4-15 shows the position after another O prints at the bottom of the column and penetrates the parabolic, switching it to the other side of the price action, marked with the red arrow.

Unlike moving averages, therefore, the Parabolic is not subject to as many whipsaw signals because it is kept away from the price immediately after a signal. This also means that the simple penetration of the Parabolic by an X or O can be used as a signal, whereas it can't with a moving average, as explained on page 46.

14　An O is said to have breached the Parabolic when the centre line of the O is below the Parabolic value. Conversely, an X is said to have breached the Parabolic when the centre line of the X is above the Parabolic value.

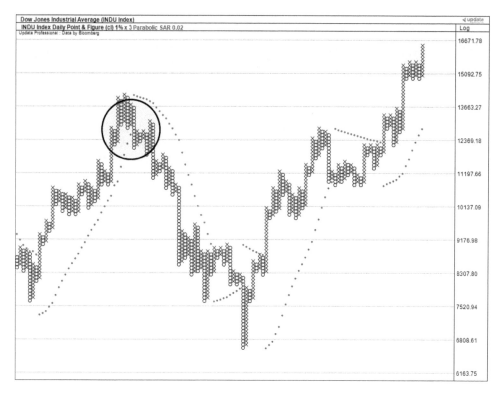

CHART 4-13: 1% X 3 OF THE DOW JONES INDUSTRIAL AVERAGE WITH A 0.02 PARABOLIC SAR

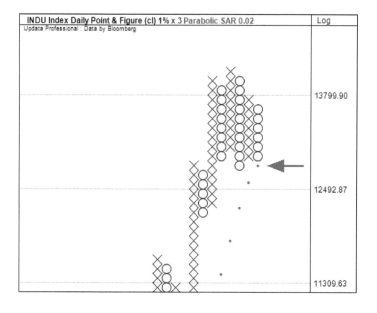

CHART 4-14: CIRCLED SECTION IN CHART 4-13 ENLARGED, SHOWING THE POSITION OF THE PARABOLIC BEFORE PENETRATION

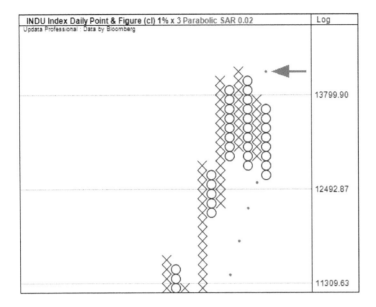

CHART 4-15: CIRCLED SECTION IN CHART 4-13 ENLARGED, SHOWING THE POSITION OF THE PARABOLIC AFTER PENETRATION

CHART 4-16: 1% X 1 OF THE DOW JONES INDUSTRIAL AVERAGE WITH A 0.02 PARABOLIC SAR

The Parabolic operates in the same way on 1-box charts, as Chart 4-16 shows, making it a very effective analysis method.

As you have seen from Chart 4-13 and Chart 4-16, the Parabolic appears simple to use.

Penetration by an X or O triggers the Parabolic to switch sides. This is one advantage the Parabolic has over moving averages – because it does not plot through the X and O columns like moving averages do, the simple penetration of the Parabolic by an X or O column can be used as a signal. This is method 1 below. There are, however, other ways to use the Parabolic with Point and Figure and these are described below, too.

Using the Parabolic with 3-box reversal charts

There are three methods for using the Parabolic to obtain alerts and signals. The first method is to use the penetration of the Parabolic by an X or O column as the signal, as shown in the charts above. The second is to use the Parabolic switch as an alert and to take the next Point and Figure signal. This is the favoured method in *The Definitive Guide to Point and Figure*. The third method is to use the penetration of the Parabolic by the column midpoint as the signal.

Method 1 – Using the penetration of the parabolic as the signal

With this method, the penetration of the bearish Parabolic by an X column, and therefore the switch from a bearish Parabolic to a bullish one, is the signal to buy. Conversely, the penetration of the bullish Parabolic by an O column, and therefore the switch from a bullish Parabolic to a bearish one, is the signal to sell. It is a clean, simple strategy and is the one shown in Charts 4-13 and 4-16, but it is not without its flaws.

Chart 4-17 shows a 3-box reversal chart with a Parabolic SAR. The first buy signal occurs at point A when a column of Xs penetrates the bearish red Parabolic. The Parabolic then switches to below the price, becoming a blue bullish Parabolic. The buy at A remains in place while the price is above the Parabolic. At point B, the blue bullish Parabolic is penetrated by a column of Os and a sell signal is generated. The Parabolic switches above the price for only two columns, then is penetrated at point C by a column of Xs, turning the Parabolic bullish again and generating a buy signal.

The Parabolic remains bullish until point D, when it is penetrated by a column of Os and the Parabolic switches to bearish again. The bearish Parabolic continues to point E, when it is penetrated by a column of Xs, turning it to bullish. The blue bullish Parabolic is penetrated by a column of Os at point F, turning it bearish again. At point G, the bearish Parabolic is penetrated by a column of Xs, turning it bullish again.

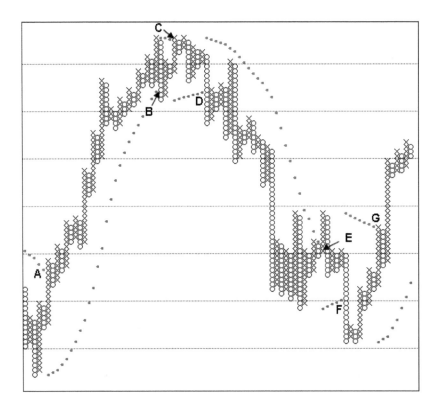

CHART 4-17: 3-BOX REVERSAL CHART SHOWING SIGNALS WHEN X OR O PENETRATES THE 0.02 PARABOLIC

Even though the parabolic starts away from the price, you can see that there are a number of bad signals or whipsaws caused by sharp moves immediately after the signals have been generated. Reducing the acceleration factor from the default 0.02 to 0.01 will delay the signals and reduce some of the whipsaws, as shown in Chart 4-18.

Whipsaws may also be reduced by using Point and Figure signals in conjunction with the Parabolic, which is method 2.

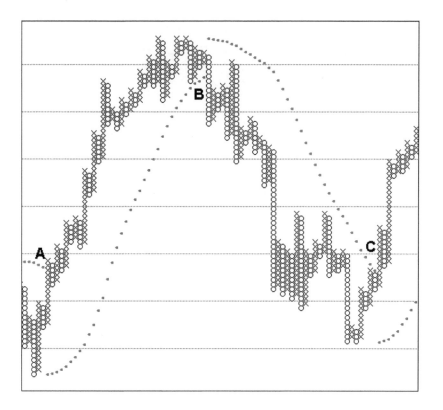

CHART 4-18: 3-BOX REVERSAL CHART SHOWING SIGNALS WHEN X OR O PENETRATES THE 0.01 PARABOLIC

Method 2 – Using the Parabolic switch as the alert to take the next Point and Figure signal

With this method, the penetration of the Parabolic by an X or O column places you on alert to look for the next Point and Figure signal. So, when an X column penetrates a bearish Parabolic switching it to bullish, you are placed on buy alert to look for the next double-top buy. If a double-top buy does not occur and a column of Os penetrates the bullish Parabolic, your buy alert is cancelled and you are placed on a sell alert to look for the next double-bottom sell. This may mean you switch from buy alert to sell alert a number of times before a signal occurs.

This method provides an additional filter to method 1, as you can see in Chart 4-19, where many of the whipsaws present with method 1 have been eliminated. The first buy signal occurs with the first double-top buy above the bullish Parabolic at point A. Signals B and C which appeared with method 1 are ignored, because there is no double-bottom sell after the penetration at point B and no double-top buy after the penetration at point C. The first sell therefore occurs at point D, with a double-bottom sell. Signals E and F in method 1 are ignored as well and the next buy signal therefore occurs with the double-top buy at point G.

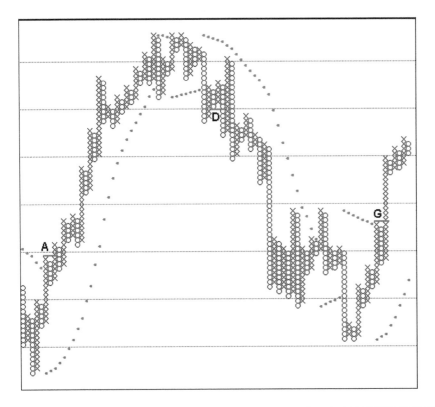

CHART 4-19: 3-BOX REVERSAL CHART SHOWING POINT AND FIGURE SIGNALS AFTER PENETRATION OF THE PARABOLIC BY X OR O

Method 3 – Using the midpoint of the column crossing the Parabolic

With this method, the penetration of the Parabolic by the midpoint of the column generates the signal by switching the Parabolic from bullish to bearish and vice versa. It is similar in concept to method 1 above, because no regard is taken of any Point and Figure signal; however, instead of the highest X and lowest O crossing the Parabolic, it is essentially the crossing of the Parabolic by a moving average, which in this case has a length of 1.

Chart 4-20 is a 3-box reversal chart with a red line tracing the midpoint of each column and a Parabolic. The first buy signal occurs at point A, when the midpoint penetrates the bearish red Parabolic. At point B, the blue bullish Parabolic is penetrated on the downside by the midpoint and a sell signal is generated. There is a buy at C, a sell at D and finally at point E a buy occurs when the midpoint penetrates the bearish Parabolic.

Compare Chart 4-20 with Chart 4-17 and notice the differences in the signals when the midpoint of the column is used instead of the high X or low O.

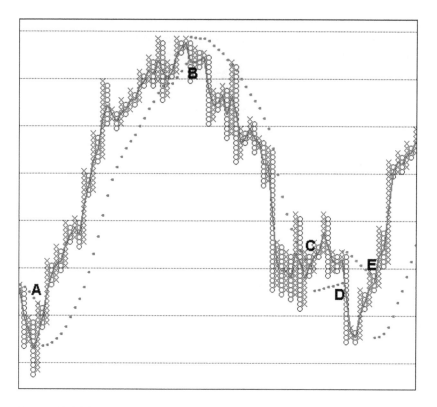

CHART 4-20: 3-BOX REVERSAL CHART SHOWING SIGNALS AFTER PENETRATION OF THE PARABOLIC BY THE MIDPOINT OF X OR O COLUMNS

Using the Parabolic with 1-box reversal charts

You will recall that the main difference in the analysis of 3-box and 1-box charts is that the patterns in 1-box charts are not as defined as those in 3-box charts. A full explanation is given on page 54, where moving averages on 1-box charts are discussed. Even so, it is possible to use all three methods that were used for 3-box charts.

Method 1 – Using the penetration of the Parabolic as the signal

As with 3-box charts, this method is the penetration of the bearish Parabolic by an X column and therefore the switch from a bearish Parabolic to a bullish one is the signal to buy. Conversely, the penetration of the bullish Parabolic by an O column and therefore the switch from a bullish Parabolic to a bearish one is the signal to sell.

1-box charts are much wider than 3-box charts, so to show the same area as that shown in the 3-box charts above, the 1-box chart has been split into Chart 4-21 and Chart 4-22.

Buy signals occur at points A, C, E, G, I, K and M, when an X penetrates the red bearish Parabolic. Sell signals occur at points B, D, F, H, J and L, when an O penetrates the blue bullish Parabolic. As you can see there are many more signals from a 1-box chart than there are from a 3-box chart because the patterns are wider and flatter. Decreasing the acceleration factor will reduce the number.

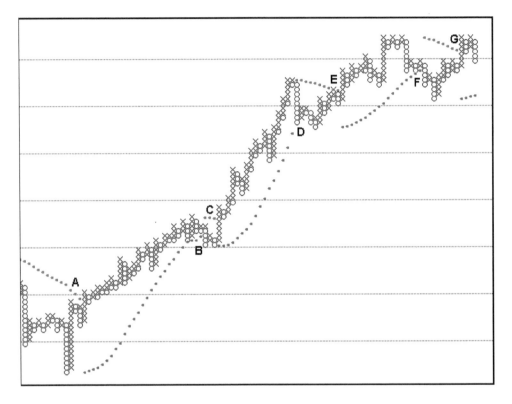

CHART 4-21: 1-BOX REVERSAL CHART SHOWING SIGNALS WHEN X OR O PENETRATES THE PARABOLIC (1 OF 2)

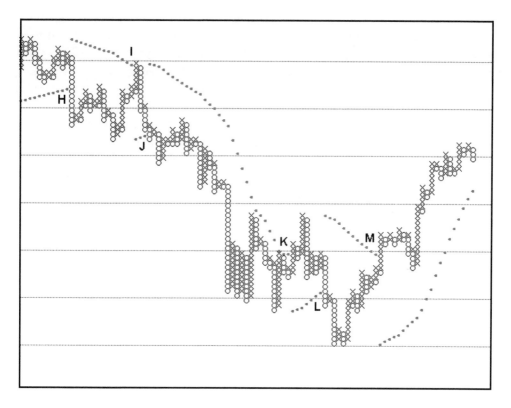

CHART 4-22: 1-BOX REVERSAL CHART SHOWING SIGNALS WHEN X OR O PENETRATES THE PARABOLIC (2 OF 2)

Method 2 – Using the Parabolic switch as the alert to take the next Point and Figure signal

With this method, the penetration of the Parabolic by an X or O column places you on alert to look for the next applicable Point and Figure signal. Remember, for the use of moving averages with 1-box charts it was decided that a buy signal occurs when an X breaks above an X in a previous column, and a sell occurs when an O breaks below an O in a previous column, rather than looking for semi-catapults and fulcrums (see page 54).

The same applies with the Parabolic, so when an X column penetrates a bearish Parabolic switching it to bullish, you are placed on buy alert to look for the next 1-box buy signal. If it occurs you buy; however, if a buy does not occur and an O column penetrates the bullish Parabolic, your buy alert is cancelled and you are placed on sell alert to look for the next 1-box sell signal. In this way you could switch from buy alert to sell alert a number of times before a signal occurs.

Chart 4-23 and Chart 4-24 show the same 1-box charts as those in method 1, with the same labelling so you can see the difference. In Chart 4-19, a buy signal occurs at point A, which is the first Point and Figure buy above the blue bullish Parabolic. At point B, a column of Os crosses below the blue bullish Parabolic switching it to red bearish and putting you on alert, but no new Point and Figure signal occurs, so there is no sell signal at B. The Parabolic turns bullish again and a second buy signal occurs at point C. This can either be ignored because you are already long, or can be taken as an 'add to position' signal. The bullish Parabolic is then penetrated by a column of Os at point D, followed a few columns later by a one-step back sell signal. The Parabolic turns bullish again when an X column penetrates it and a buy is registered at point E, followed by a sell at point F. There is, however, no buy at point G because there is no Point and Figure signal above the blue Parabolic.

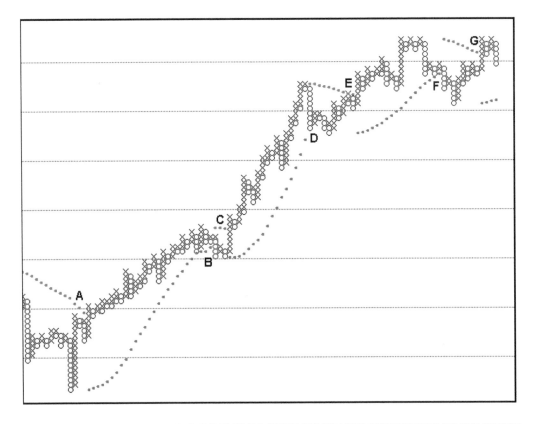

CHART 4-23: 1-BOX REVERSAL CHART SHOWING POINT AND FIGURE SIGNALS AFTER PENETRATION OF THE PARABOLIC BY X OR O (1 OF 2)

In Chart 4-24 there is a repeat sell at point H. At this stage you are already out of the market or short following the sell signal at point F, so you may either ignore the new sell or add to a short position. Although point I is above the bullish Parabolic there is no 1-box signal, so therefore no buy. There is a second repeat sell at point J, meaning that since the buy at point E, there have been three sell signals – F, H and J – with no buy signal between them. A buy then occurs at point K, followed by a sell at point L, followed by a buy at point M.

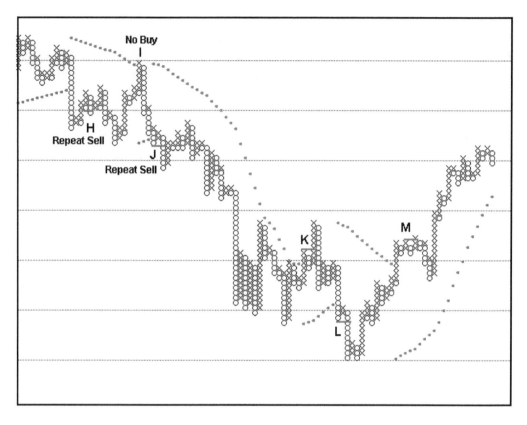

CHART 4-24: 1-BOX REVERSAL CHART SHOWING POINT AND FIGURE SIGNALS AFTER PENETRATION OF THE PARABOLIC BY X OR O (2 OF 2)

Using the additional filter of the Point and Figure signal changes the position of the signals and eliminates some signals.

Method 3 – Using the midpoint of the column crossing the Parabolic

With this method, the penetration of the Parabolic by the midpoint of the column generates the signal by switching the Parabolic from bullish to bearish and vice versa. It is similar in concept to method 1 above, because no regard is taken of any Point and Figure signal and instead of the highest X and lowest O crossing the Parabolic, it is essentially the crossing of the Parabolic by a moving average, which in this case has a length of 1.

The clearest way to show this is to remove the Point and Figure chart and draw the midpoint column line with the Parabolic. Remember, with this method the Point and Figure chart itself plays no part in the signals, although it has played a part in the calculation of the Parabolic and the midpoint column line. Chart 4-25 and Chart 4-26 show the same section as before, allowing you to see exactly where the buy and sell signals occurred.

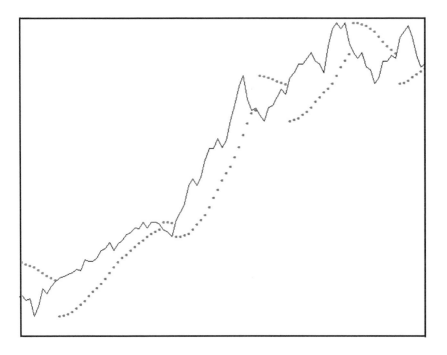

CHART 4-25: MIDPOINT OF 1-BOX REVERSAL CHART SHOWING SIGNALS AFTER PENETRATION OF THE PARABOLIC (1 OF 2)

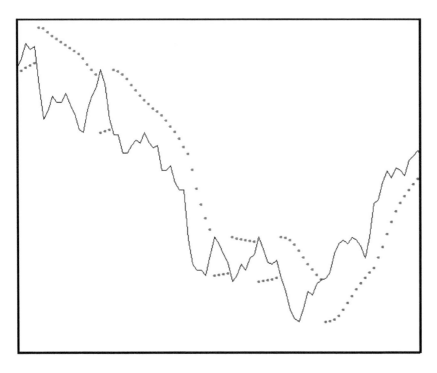

CHART 4-26: MIDPOINT OF 1-BOX REVERSAL CHART SHOWING SIGNALS AFTER PENETRATION OF THE PARABOLIC (2 OF 2)

Other ways of using the Parabolic

You have seen that the interaction of the Parabolic with the midpoint column value is one of the methods presented. Because the midpoint value is simply a 1 column moving average, you could choose any other length for the moving average and use the reaction of that moving average with the Parabolic.

You have also seen, when Donchian channels and Bollinger bands were discussed, that instead of looking for Point and Figure signals, you could look for breaks above or below the columns that breach the Parabolic rather than actual Point and Figure signals.

Parabolic acceleration factor

The Parabolic acceleration factor determines the speed with which the Parabolic accelerates towards the price. The original default acceleration factor is 0.02, but that may be modified. The smaller the factor, the further away from the price action and the slower the Parabolic is in catching up to the price. This is the equivalent of using a longer-length moving average. You should therefore reduce the factor when adding the Parabolic to 1-box reversal charts and those using the high/low, low/high and ohlc construction because the patterns are wider. Chart 4-27 shows three Parabolic SARs. The closest to the price action is the 0.02, then the 0.01, then the 0.005.

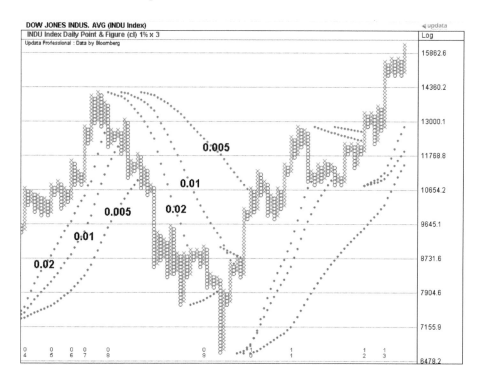

CHART 4-27: 1% X 3 OF THE DOW JONES INDUSTRIAL AVERAGE WITH 0.02, 0.01 AND 0.005 PARABOLIC SARS

SUMMARY

This chapter has expanded on Chapter 3 by exploring three other tools that can be used on Point and Figure charts to identify trend and from which buy and sell signals can be generated. Donchian channels, Bollinger bands and Parabolic SAR each have a slightly different way of being used, but they all define trend and identify turning points.

Donchian channels mark the highest X and lowest O over a defined number of columns and in doing so define uptrends and downtrends in a similar way to moving average and 45° trend lines. In addition, it has been shown how breaks above or below the defined levels can be used to make buy and sell decisions.

Bollinger bands, a popular tool amongst time-based chart users, can be used with Point and Figure by following the same calculation method as that used for moving averages. The bands are based on volatility and so expand and contract as volatility changes. They show areas of strong trend and low volatility. In a similar way to Donchian channels, Bollinger bands can be used in the generation of buy and sell signals, although this is not how they are used with time-based charts.

Wilder's Parabolic SAR defines trends in a similar way to 45° trend lines where the trend is either up or down and buy and sell signals can be generated in a similar way to those obtained from moving averages.

Chapter Five. Indicators of Point and Figure Charts

INTRODUCTION

THIS CHAPTER IS DELIBERATELY ENTITLED 'INDICATORS *OF* POINT and Figure Charts' because the indicators are calculated from the Point and Figure chart and not from the raw data, which is the case for indicators used with time-based charts. The Point and Figure chart must be drawn first, then the indicator calculated using the same technique as that used to calculate moving averages in the previous chapter; that is the midpoint of each column is the proxy for the column and is therefore used to calculate the indicator using the number of columns as the length.

This means that a change in the Point and Figure parameters and construction method will result in a different Point and Figure chart and consequently a different looking indicator. It is nothing to be alarmed about. The Point and Figure chart comes first. Once you are satisfied with the parameters you have used to draw the Point and Figure chart, you may then add an indicator calculated off the chart itself.

The idea that technical indicators could be used with Point and Figure charts was first made public in my chapter entitled 'Point and Figure Analysis: Modern Developments in an Old Technique' in the 2007 book, *Breakthroughs in Technical Analysis*, edited by David Keller. It has made Point and Figure charts even more attractive as an analysis method than they were before. Because charts like line, bar and candle had time scales, they took part in the proliferation of calculated indicators that emerged when the PC became the tool for technical analysis, leaving Point and Figure charts behind in this development. That is no longer the case – any calculated indicator may now be used on Point and Figure charts.

Where indicators such as OBOS,[15] MACD,[16] RSI,[17] etc., use the time-based bar's close price, in the case of Point and Figure the midpoint of each column is used as the proxy value to

---

15 Overbought/oversold.
16 Moving Average Convergence Divergence devised by Gerald Appel.
17 Relative Strength Index devised by J. Welles Wilder.

calculate the indicator. Where indicators such as Stochastic[18] and Directional Movement[19] use the time-based bar's high and low, in the case of Point and Figure they use the column's high and low and, if required, use the midpoint of the column for the close.

Although any calculated indicator can be applied to Point and Figure charts, only a few are covered here for reasons of brevity. This is not a recommendation of which indicator to use but rather they are chosen because either they are in common use, or there is some difference in reading them with Point and Figure charts.

This book can't go into detail about what these indicators are, or how each is calculated. That is a whole subject on its own and you should refer to the original works for more details of each indicator. The assumption is that you know what these indicators are and how they are used with time-based charts, because much is similar with Point and Figure and any differences will be explained. As with moving averages, indicators should be calculated off log scale Point and Figure charts in order to keep the sensitivity throughout the chart the same.

There are a number of reasons why technical analysts use indicators. They show whether the price is overbought or oversold, meaning whether it has risen or fallen too far, too fast; they help to confirm or reject the price trend by observing whether the oscillator is diverging from the price chart; and they are used simply to generate buy and sell signals according to a set of rules, which could be penetration of levels, moving average crossovers or some other rule. Because in Point and Figure terms they are calculated from the Point and Figure chart, they show whether the Point and Figure chart is overbought or oversold or whether there is divergence between the Point and Figure chart and the indicator.

Understanding Divergence

Divergence is an important part of using any indicator but is often misunderstood, so a brief description is necessary. The most important thing to understand is occurrence of divergence is not a buy or sell signal, rather it is a warning that something is not right and that you should be on alert. Divergence can take place over a few minutes, days or years. Divergence between the price and an indicator occurs in two ways: when the price makes a new low, but the indicator does not (bullish divergence) or when the price makes a new high and the indicator does not (bearish divergence). Divergence points to strength or weakness in the underlying price trend.

In order to help you understand the concept, consider the analogy of a vehicle in motion up a hill. You look at the speedometer and notice that the speed is starting to fall. You look out of the window and happily you are still going up the hill. As the vehicle continues forward, however, the speed continues to fall, and you realise that perhaps the vehicle won't make it to the top. The reduction in speed is a warning to you that there is something wrong and if you were travelling in that vehicle, you may choose to continue or stop and get out before

18 Stochastic devised by George Lane.
19 Directional Movement Index devised by J, Welles Wilder.

it runs back down the hill. Substitute the word instrument for vehicle, price for distance travelled and oscillator for speed of travel. A rising price combined with a falling oscillator is your warning that something is wrong.

Displaying Indicators with Point and Figure Charts

Point and Figure charts are drawn on a squared grid which means that often they flow off the top or bottom of the chart window. A chart showing a lot of history means it is tall as well, leaving little room to show a line chart of the indicator below the Point and Figure chart. For this reason, when drawing Point and Figure charts with indicators the only way to show as much history as possible without losing part of the chart below the level of the window is to reduce the physical size of the Xs and Os. This makes it difficult to see Point and Figure patterns but makes the indicators themselves more readable.

OVERBOUGHT/OVERSOLD OSCILLATOR (OBOS)

Although there are a number of interpretations of what an overbought/oversold oscillator is, the one used here is closely related to moving averages, because it measures the distance between the price and a moving average.

To calculate the OBOS, therefore, you must draw a moving average on the Point and Figure chart, then calculate the distance from the moving average to the last X in each X column and from the moving average to the last O in each O column. The OBOS therefore has a zigzag shape, oscillating between the X at the top and the O at the bottom of each column. The value of the OBOS is the points value represented by that number of Xs or Os above or below the moving average. Because the Point and Figure chart is log scaled, each X and O represents a slightly different value. The OBOS itself may be plotted as an absolute value, which is the number of points above or below the moving average, or as the percentage by which the X or O is away from the moving average. A rising OBOS chart means that the gap between the columns and the moving average is increasing and so is bullish.

Chart 5-1 is a 1% x 3 of the S&P 500 with two 10 column OBOS indicators. The first is calculated on absolute differences (labelled 'abs') and the second on percentage differences. As stated above, the physical size of the Xs and Os has been reduced to keep the Point and Figure chart condensed and so enable the OBOS indicators to be shown over sufficient history. You will see there are minor differences in shape between the two OBOS indicators.

The most important reason to use the OBOS indicator is to show how overbought or oversold the chart is, which means how far the X and O columns are above or below the moving average. This is done by looking back over the history to see where the past turning points in the oscillator have occurred. The centre chart in Chart 5-1 is the absolute OBOS and there you will see that turning points occur at +250 points and -250 points. In the bottom chart, the percentage OBOS chart, they occur at +20% and -20%. These are the extremes; however, it is possible that these levels can be exceeded or, conversely, never achieved again. There is no reason why they shouldn't be exceeded, or not achieved at all.

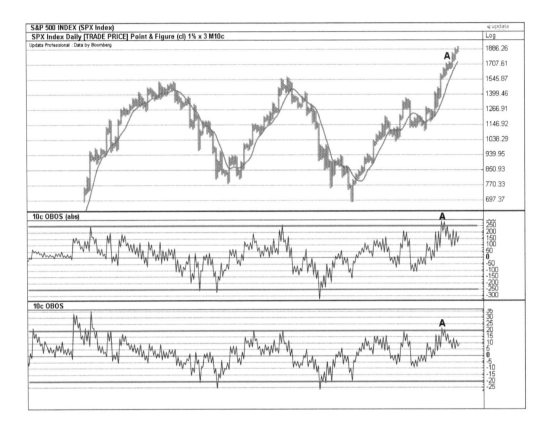

CHART 5-1: 1% X 3 OF S&P 500 WITH 10 COLUMN OBOS BASED ON ABSOLUTE AND PERCENTAGE DIFFERENCES

Overbought and oversold does not mean sell and buy respectively; if anything it means *don't* buy and *don't* sell. If the trend is up, as the current trend is in Chart 5-1, the overbought level reached at point A tells you that the strength of the trend has reached its limit and that additional Point and Figure buy signals should be treated with caution until the overboughtness has subsided. Obviously if the trend continues, as it has in this case, any existing holdings will benefit from the continuing trend. Reaching oversold levels in a downtrend is a good time to stop selling and to close any shorts. So it is important that these levels are used in conjunction with the underlying price trend. They help to put you in the right frame of mind, either buying or selling.

Divergences tend to show up better when percentage OBOS is used because it automatically adjusts to the price level; however, you will see divergences on both styles of OBOS. Chart 5-2 shows a 1% x 3 chart of the S&P 500 again with a 10 column OBOS with divergences and confirmations marked. You can see that bearish divergence occurred between A&B, E&F, F&G and N&O, and bullish divergence occurred between C&D, H&I and L&M. Divergence is a warning and can last between 4 or 5 columns (as in the case of F&G), or over 50 columns (as in the case of A&B). This demonstrates that divergence cannot be used as an entry or exit signal, but rather as a warning.

Not every top and bottom has divergence. Sometimes there is confirmation, as is the case between J&K. This shows that everything is in place when the high is made. Normally confirmation would result in a continuation of the trend but in the case of J&K something unforeseen caused the price to fall sharply to L.

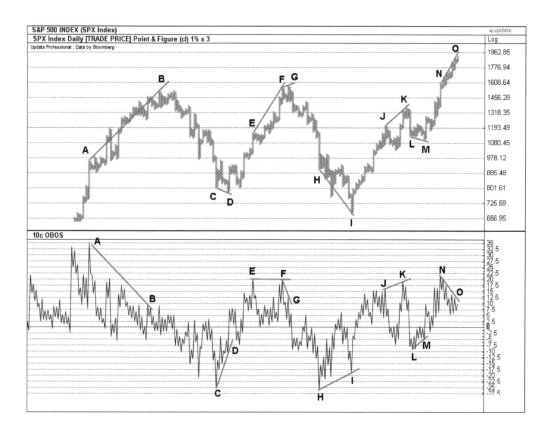

CHART 5-2: 1% X 3 OF S&P 500 WITH 10 COLUMN OBOS SHOWING DIVERGENCE

OBOS is not confined to 3-box charts and daily data, it can be used with any reversal and any time frame data. Chart 5-3 is a 60 minute 0.1% x 1 chart of Brent Crude with a 10 column OBOS below. Notice that +1% and -1% are typical overbought and oversold levels. Some divergences are also marked on the chart.

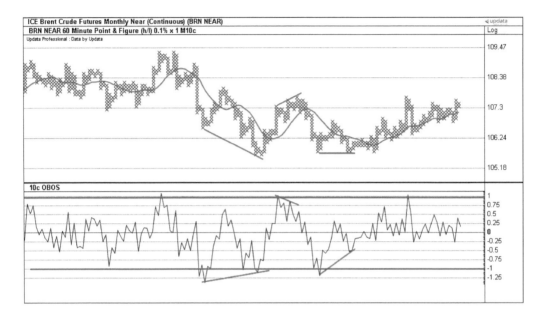

CHART 5-3: 0.1% X 1 OF BRENT CRUDE WITH 10 COLUMN OBOS SHOWING DIVERGENCE

MOVING AVERAGE CONVERGENCE/DIVERGENCE (MACD)

MACD is a popular indicator amongst time-based chart users. It is ideally suited for adaptation to Point and Figure because it simply measures the difference between two moving averages and you have already seen how easy it is to calculate a moving average of a Point and Figure chart. Traditionally MACD is calculated off exponential moving averages, but there is no reason why simple or any other moving average calculation can't be used.

Because of the way MACD is calculated, there is a direct relationship between MACD and the moving averages covered in Chapter 3. You will recall that method 2 used the penetration of the moving average by the midpoint column value as the signal to buy and sell. Chart 5-4 is a 1% x 3 of the S&P 500 with 1 column (red) and 20 column (blue) exponential moving averages. Below is a 20,1 MACD, based on the same two moving averages, showing the difference between the 20 column moving average and midpoint of each column. When the midpoint of the column crosses the 20 column moving average, the MACD crosses the zero line.

Like the OBOS discussed in the previous section and many other oscillators, the MACD shows when the Point and Figure chart is overbought and oversold. It can also show divergence, but that is less apparent because of its smoothness. What it does do with the combination of MACD and a signal line is to provide entry and exit points. As with all indicators that provide entry and exit signals, the signal is the alert to take the next Point and Figure signal. In addition, MACD also tells you what the underlying trend is; MACD above the zero means the chart is in an uptrend and below the zero means the chart is in a downtrend.

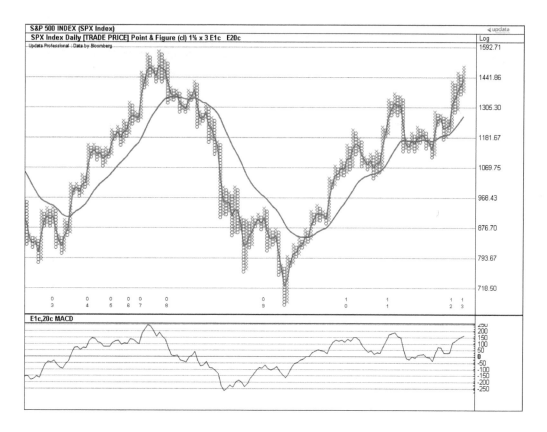

CHART 5-4: 1% X 3 OF THE S&P 500 WITH 1 COLUMN AND 20 COLUMN MOVING AVERAGE AND 20,1 MACD

One thing you will notice when using MACD is that the standard settings of 26,12 with a 9 signal line appear to work best with Point and Figure charts as they do with other charts. The Euro Bund future has been in a solid uptrend (falling interest rates) for over 20 years, as shown by Chart 5-5, which is a 0.5% x 3 of the Euro Bund[20] with a standard length 26,12 column MACD below.

The 45° lines on the Point and Figure chart show the strong uptrend, but during that uptrend there have been excellent buying opportunities each time there is a breakout from a fulcrum pattern. One of the purposes of using indicators like the MACD is to assist with deciding whether a breakout is valid or not. In this case, each time a fulcrum pattern is about to break out, the MACD crosses up through its signal line, giving you confidence to act. The MACD entry points are shown by the vertical blue lines on the chart and coincide well with the fulcrum breakouts. When the MACD signal occurs, it puts you on alert to take the next Point and Figure double-top buy signal or, if you prefer, to wait for the full fulcrum breakout.

20 The Euro Bund future chart has been rollover adjusted to preserve the trend. For more information, see the article on the subject of adjusting contracts in the references section.

As well as providing entry alerts, the MACD also provides exit alerts when it crosses below its signal line. This is shown by the red vertical lines. Exit signals during an uptrend mean that buying should cease and some profits should be taken. They do not mean that trend has changed. Although the corrections have not been deep, some have lasted two or more years, during which time other investments may have been performing.

CHART 5-5: 0.5% X 3 OF EURO BUND FUTURE WITH 26,12C MACD WITH 9C SIGNAL LINE SHOWING SIGNALS

MACD enhances the reading of 1-box charts in the same way as it does 3-box charts, but because 1-box charts are more subjective, the MACD is of more assistance. Chart 5-6 is a 1% x 1 chart of the US 10 Year Yield showing about six years of data. Below is a standard 26,12 MACD with a 9 column signal line.

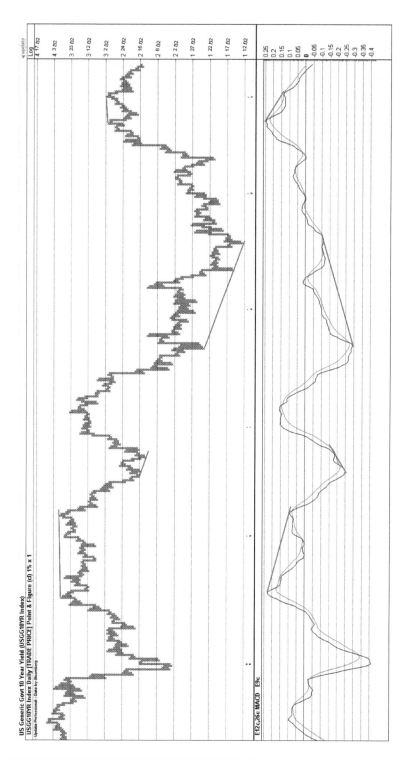

CHART 5-6: 1% X 1 OF US 10 YEAR YIELD WITH 26,12C MACD SHOWING DIVERGENCE AND WITH A 9C SIGNAL LINE

Place a sheet of paper over the MACD in Chart 5-6, leaving just the Point and Figure chart, and see whether you can analyse the chart with certainty. It is worth spending some time doing so. Then expose the MACD and notice the 1-box chart becomes much more readable. Firstly, areas where turning points occur are easier to spot because the MACD is crossing its signal line. The main price trends are easier to spot by observing when the MACD crosses above and below the zero line. Areas where perhaps you were unsure are confirmed or rejected by observing the MACD. Finally, although MACD does not always show divergences, there are some important ones marked with blue lines on the chart.

Adding the MACD reduces the confusion often seen on very short-term charts. Chart 5-7 is a 1 minute 0.1% x 3 chart of Henry Hub Natural Gas with a standard length MACD below. Once again, the turning points in what is a volatile chart are easy to see with the assistance of the MACD. Notice that the analysis of whipsaw changes in the 45° trend (circled) is made easier by observing the MACD, which remains in an uptrend at that point.

CHART 5-7: 1 MINUTE 0.1% X 3 OF HENRY HUB NATURAL GAS WITH 26,12C MACD

Adding MACD Histogram

Closely associated to MACD is the MACD Histogram, which plots the difference between MACD and its signal line, and is normally plotted as a histogram style chart, hence its name. When the MACD crosses its signal line, the MACD Histogram crosses through zero. The MACD Histogram is an early warning chart because it peaks when the gap between MACD and its signal line is at its largest. It can either be plotted on its own or overlaid on the MACD as shown in the lower window in Chart 5-8. You can see the MACD Histogram has gone from blue to red, showing that it has crossed the zero line, which means the MACD has crossed its signal line.

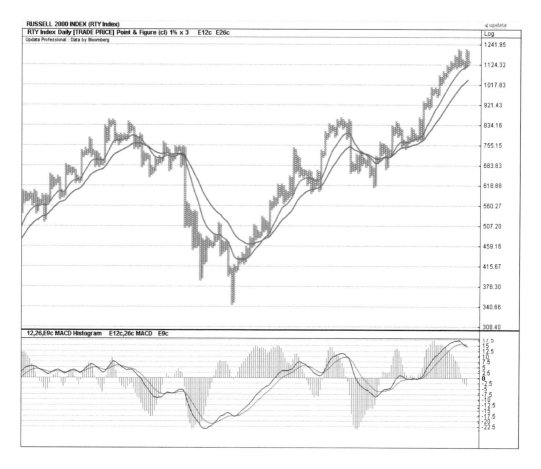

CHART 5-8: 1% X 3 CHART OF THE RUSSELL 2000 WITH 12 AND 26 COLUMN EXPONENTIAL MOVING AVERAGES AND 12,26 MACD OVERLAYED ON A 12,26 MACD HISTOGRAM

RELATIVE STRENGTH INDEX (RSI)

Welles Wilder's RSI is another very popular indicator in the Technical Analysis world, used by most analysts in conjunction with their candle or bar charts. It is a momentum based indicator, meaning that it is a rate of change indicator. For Point and Figure charts it is calculated from the midpoint column value and so it has a smoother appearance than the time-based version.

One of its advantages is that it has a fixed scale range from 0 to 100, which makes it more readable than the MACD and OBOS covered above. Like all other oscillators, RSI tells you if the chart is overbought or oversold and whether there is divergence.

The standard RSI length is 14 periods, but you may wish to halve that and start with 7 columns. Chart 5-9 is a daily 0.25% x 3 chart of the British Pound (Cable), with a 7 column RSI below. It is traditional to regard the RSI above 70 as overbought and below 30 as oversold. Breaks below 70 and above 30 are often regarded as sell and buy signals, with the 50 level being the level at which the trend changes. In the case of Point and Figure, you should use breaks from above 70 and below 30 as alerts. Instead of 45° trend lines, a 10 column moving average has been drawn on the Point and Figure chart to highlight the trends.

Positive and negative divergences are marked with red diagonal lines on both charts; positive divergence where the price makes a new low but the RSI does not, and negative divergence where the price makes a new high and the RSI does not. These do not occur at every turning point, but when they do, they are an additional alert to a trend change.

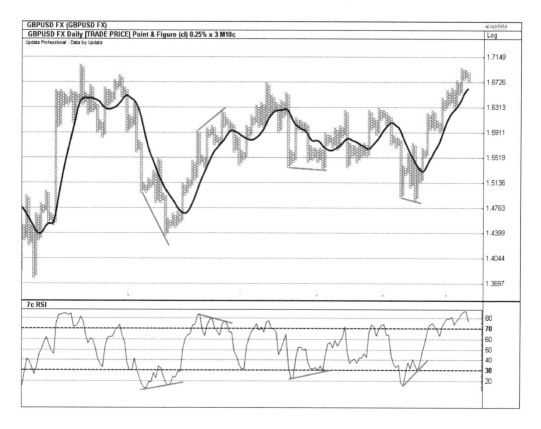

CHART 5-9: 0.25% X 3 OF GBPUSD WITH 7 COLUMN RSI SHOWING DIVERGENCE

Chart 5-10 is a 60 minute 0.25% x 3 chart of gold with a 14 column RSI below, showing about a year of data. Notice that on two occasions when the RSI rose above 70, then broke below, these were both important tops with a break of the 45° trend line following shortly after that. Notice too that breaks above 30 have signalled important lows.

CHART 5-10: HOURLY 0.25% X 3 OF GOLD WITH 14 COLUMN RSI

DIRECTIONAL MOVEMENT

Directional Movement is another Welles Wilder indicator and is different from the oscillators discussed so far in that it is a three-line indicator, one measuring the strength of the trend and the other two defining whether the trend is up or down. It has a fixed scale range of 0 to 100, but it is not an overbought/oversold oscillator in the true sense.

Essentially what Directional Movement does is decompose the trend into a positive (+DI) and negative (-DI) component which are then plotted together. When +DI exceeds -DI the trend is up and when -DI exceeds +DI the trend is down. The strength of the trend is then measured by a third line called ADX, although ADX does not indicate trend direction. Directional Movement is a very easy indicator to read and works well with Point and Figure charts with its standard length of 14 columns.

Chart 5-11 is a 2% x 3 of American Express Company with a 14 column Directional Movement below. Changes in trend are signalled when the blue +DI and red -DI cross one another and these are marked with vertical blue and red lines on the chart. Notice how these changes in trend coincide with the 45° trend changes on the Point and Figure chart. The green ADX line measures the strength of the trend defined by the position of +DI and -DI, however, the position of +DI and -DI is less important when the ADX line is below 25, indicating that the Point and Figure chart is not trending. The strength of the trend is currently the highest it has been and the gap between +DI and -DI is the greatest it has been. The greater the gap, the more overbought or oversold the Point and Figure chart.

CHART 5-11: 2% X 3 OF AMERICAN EXPRESS WITH 14 COLUMN DIRECTIONAL MOVEMENT

Sometimes Directional Movement can be used to forewarn of a trend change, allowing you to start reducing positions ahead of the change. Chart 5-12 is the NASDAQ 100 with a 14 column Directional Movement. Although +DI and -DI crosses marked A, B & C coincide with 45° trend changes, the cross marked D occurs long before the main bullish 45° trend line from the 1991 low is breached. The early Directional Movement signal puts you on alert to consider acting earlier, based on breaks of the internal 45° lines instead. Notice that throughout the chart, the green ADX line remains above 25, indicating that the market is trending both ways and that signals from +DI and -DI should not be ignored.

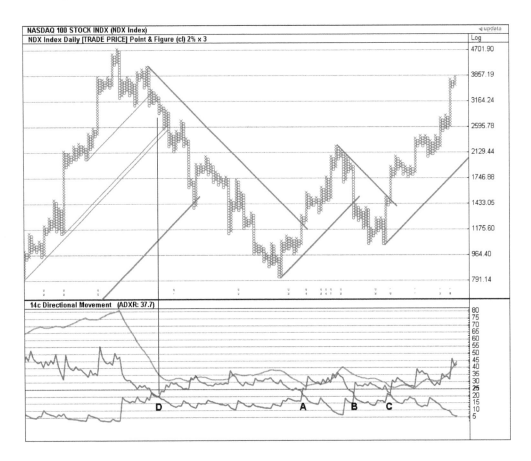

CHART 5-12: 2% X 3 OF THE NASDAQ 100 WITH 14 COLUMN DIRECTIONAL MOVEMENT

Chart 5-13 is a 60 minute 0.12% x 3 chart of the Copper Future with a 14 column Directional Movement below. Notice that the red -DI crossed above the blue +DI signifying a downtrend before the sharp decline on the left of the chart. This coincided with the break of the 45° uptrend, thus confirming the break.

CHART 5-13: HOURLY 0.12% X 3 OF COPPER FUTURE WITH 9 COLUMN DIRECTIONAL MOVEMENT

INDEXIA MARKET TRACKER

The Indexia Market Tracker[21] is a proprietary indicator, so perhaps discussing it without divulging any information about its calculation may be inappropriate, but because its performance on Point and Figure is so good, the temptation is too great not to. Those who do not agree may skip this section.

The Indexia Market Tracker is unique because it is a trend following oscillator, which may seem a contradiction in terms, but it means a single line defines trend as well as overbought and oversold. Standard use overbought/oversold indicators are momentum based and so can turn down even though the trend is continuing.

The Market Tracker benefits from a fixed scale range between -100 and +100, where +100 is the overbought extreme and -100 is the oversold extreme. Because it is a trend following oscillator, it does not show divergence because divergence can only occur when the trend is not part of the oscillator. Although it was designed initially for time-based charts, it is discussed here because of its clean lines and how well it works with Point and Figure charts. No other oscillator looks like it, or performs like it.

The zero line is the border line between the main up trend and main down trend. If the Market Tracker is in the positive area, the main trend is up, and if it is in the negative area the main trend is down. Within these positive and negative areas, minor trends will be changing from up to down and vice versa. Being a trend following indicator, the Market Tracker will trace out those trends within the main trend areas.

In order to calculate the Market Tracker, a parameter of the number of columns is required. Like moving averages, this parameter defines the level of trend being exposed. Decreasing the length exposes more of the minor trends and reduces the time horizon of the main trend.

Although the Market Tracker does not actually calculate probabilities, it can be thought of as a probability indicator because the scale of 0 to +100 measures the extent to which the price is overbought and 0 to -100 measures the extent to which it is oversold. The further away it is from the zero line, the more overbought or oversold is the Point and Figure chart, and therefore the higher the probability of a reversal. Because the Market Tracker gives this indication, it helps to avoid the problem of buying at the top and selling at the bottom. Normally when the Market Tracker is above +75, buying should cease, but provided it remains above +75, the uptrend is intact and you should hold positions. The Market Tracker can remain above +75 for some time, which simply means the uptrend is being maintained. A break below +75 indicates that the trend is deteriorating and can therefore be regarded as an alert. In Point and Figure terms that means wait for the next Point and Figure double-bottom sell. Because the signal occurs in the positive area, it is an early and therefore minor sell signal against the main up trend.

---

21 The Indexia Market Tracker is proprietary and was created in the early 1980s by Jeremy du Plessis whilst running Indexia Research Limited. It was previously only available in Indexia software but is now available in Updata software.

The converse is true when the Market Tracker is below -75. Selling should cease but you should continue to hold short positions while it remains below -75 because it means the downtrend is still intact. A break above -75 indicates the downtrend starting to turn positive so shorts should be covered on the next Point and Figure buy signal. Because the signal occurs in the negative area, it is an early cover buy signal against the main down trend and therefore a minor signal.

So what the Market Tracker does is put you in the right frame of mind. Below -75 you are in a buying frame of mind, waiting for the alert to look for buy signals, and above +75 you are in a selling frame of mind, waiting for the alert to look for sell signals. These levels can of course be adjusted to suit the instrument you are looking at.

Chart 5-14 is a 1% x 3 of the S&P 500 with a 13 column Market Tracker. The first thing to notice is that, compared to the other indicators covered, the Market Tracker is smooth and clear. Notice the selling areas above +75 and buying areas below -75. Breaks down through +75 are shown by the thin red lines and breaks down through zero, which signify a main trend change, are shown by thick red lines. The thin blue lines show breaks up from below -75 and the thick blue lines show breaks up through zero. Notice how the zero line crosses shown by the thick lines coincide with the 45° trend line breaks. Notice too how the Market Tracker found support on the zero line at the same time as it found support on the 45° uptrend line.

The Market Tracker gives you a summary of what the state of the Point and Figure chart is at any time. It firstly tells you what the main trend is – uptrend if Market Tracker is above zero and downtrend if it is below zero. In the example above, these trends are also marked out by the 45° trend lines, although that may not always be the case. Secondly, the Market Tracker tells you the direction of the minor trends by the direction in which the Market Tracker is moving. A rising Market Tracker means the minor trend is up, a falling Market Tracker means the minor trend is down. If the Market Tracker is rising in the negative area, it means the price is moving up against the main downtrend. Conversely, if it is falling in the positive area, it means the price is moving down against the main uptrend. Remember that prior to any main trend change, the minor trend must have moved in the opposite direction to it in order for the main trend to eventually change.

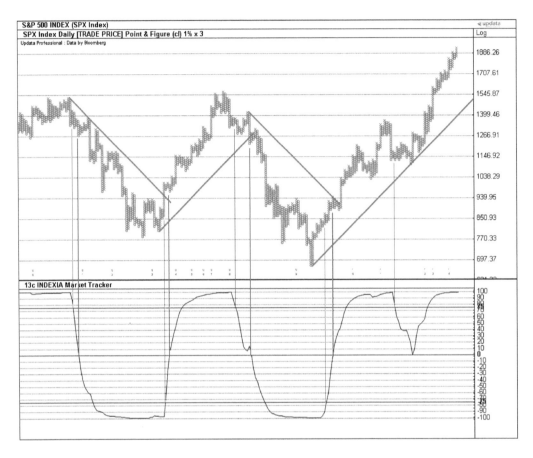

CHART 5-14: 1% X 3 OF THE S&P 500 WITH 13 COLUMN INDEXIA MARKET TRACKER

The Market Tracker is especially useful with 1-box reversal charts, where any analysis of the Point and Figure chart is more subjective than that on 3-box charts. Chart 5-15 is a 1 minute 0.05% x 1 chart of the S&P 500 with a 13 column Market Tracker showing approximately 1 month of data. Place a sheet of paper over the Market Tracker and look only at the 1-box Point and Figure chart and see if you can spot the turning points. Then expose the Market Tracker and you will see how it enhances the 1-box chart and clearly defines the turning points and main trend changes.

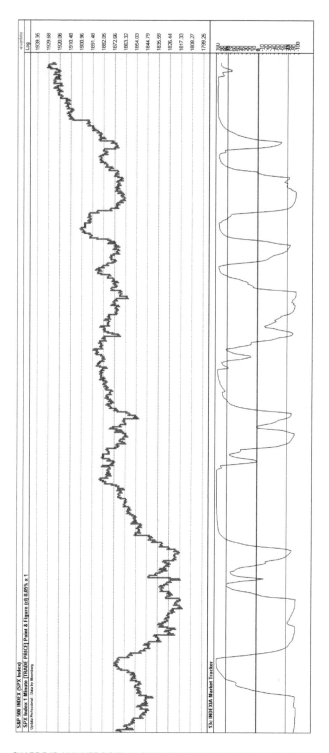

CHART 5-15: 1 MINUTE 0.05% X 1 OF THE S&P 500 WITH 13 COLUMN INDEXIA MARKET TRACKER

SUMMARY

The ability to use indicators calculated from the Point and Figure chart and drawn below it has enhanced the reading of the charts and provides you with more information than has ever been available before. It has allowed Point and Figure to participate in the proliferation of calculated indicators which, in the past, has been the preserve of time-based charts. These indicators allow you to see instantly whether the Point and Figure chart is overbought or oversold and they allow you to see divergence warnings about new highs and new lows not being confirmed. This has changed the analysis of Point and Figure charts forever.

The indicators covered here are by no means exhaustive – there are thousands of indicators available and these can be read and used in much the same way as those discussed here. The few indicators discussed here will give you some idea about how indicators generally can be used with Point and Figure charts and help you to decide whether they are worth using with your charts. The interesting thing about indicators is that different analysts prefer different ones. Some prefer the sharp moving ones like Momentum, OBOS or RSI, others prefer the smooth ones, like MACD, Stochastic or the Indexia Market Tracker. You should not forget the Directional Movement Index discussed here as well. You are encouraged to try your favourite indicator with Point and Figure – it will enhance your analysis.

You will notice that the close only construction was used in the charts of this chapter. That was more for convenience than anything else. If you choose to draw high/low or low/high Point and Figure charts instead, these will have wider patterns and so you will need to lengthen your indicator parameters.

Chapter Six. Volume on Point and Figure Charts

INTRODUCTION

VOLUME IS IMPORTANT IN TECHNICAL ANALYSIS BECAUSE IT TELLS you the amount of interest there is in any price move. A price rising on high volume warrants more attention than one rising on low volume.

That Point and Figure charts take no account of volume is a basic tenet of Point and Figure charting laid down a hundred years ago. It is not that Point and Figure analysts prefer not to have volume, it is that traditionally there has been no room for volume in a Point and Figure chart. This traditional inability to show volume has been the source of one of the criticisms levelled at the method, but it is no longer the case today.

Volume can be shown in three ways on Point and Figure charts: column volume which shows the volume in each column; volume at price which shows the volume at each box level; and volume indicators, such as On-balance volume (OBV),[22] Volume-Price Trend[23] and others.

COLUMN VOLUME

Just as a vertical volume histogram is drawn below a bar chart to show the amount of volume behind each bar, so a volume histogram can be drawn below each Point and Figure column to show how much volume there is behind the column. But it is not quite as simple as adding up all the volume from the start date of the column to the end date, because some of that volume could be volume when the price was moving in the opposite direction to the column, although not sufficient enough to cause a reversal.

So summing all the volume in an X column, for example, would give a false impression of the volume associated with building the column, if some of it was on days, hours, minutes,

---

22 On-balance volume was devised by Joseph Granville and published in his 1963 book, *Granville's New Key to Stock Market Profits*.
23 Volume-Price Trend was devised by David Markstein and published in his 1966 book, *How to Chart your way to Stock Market Profits*.

etc., when the price was moving against the column. Remember that a column could take a long time to form.

Some have suggested that you should subtract the volume on those days, but that could result in the column volume figure for the last column decreasing in length as time passes. This would make analysis impossible, because what may look high volume in the column one day may be reduced significantly by high volume in the opposite direction a week later. This would mean that the column and its volume could only be realistically evaluated once the column length had been fixed by a reversal, which could mean waiting a long time before any analysis could be completed.

One of the important aspects of Point and Figure charts is the 'effort' required to print a new box. In fact, Point and Figure analysis is based on the building of new boxes in columns and the reversals against them. All other price movement below the box and reversal variables is ignored and so it must be with volume. The volume in any column, therefore, is the sum of the volumes that created new boxes – all other volume is ignored. This means that each time a new box is plotted, the volume associated with that box is added to the running total for the column. This ensures that the volume histogram only reflects volume that increased the length of the column and, more importantly, cannot decrease as the column builds.

Chart 6-1 is a 1% x 3 Henry Hub Natural Gas futures contract. Below the Point and Figure chart is the column volume histogram showing the summation of the volume required to print a new box in each column. Notice at a glance that the red O column volumes dominate in the downtrend between points A and B, whereas the blue X column volumes dominate in the uptrend between points B and C. That is to be expected, but the key to analysing volume is when this stops occurring, in other words when the volume behind the column does not match the expectation.

Although generally the longer the X and O column the greater the volume histogram, this is not always the case. Sometimes long columns of Xs and Os have lower volume and sometimes short columns can have higher volume. When high volume occurs in short columns, it tells you that there is strong interest, which increases the column's importance even though it is short.

CHART 6-1: 1% X 3 HENRY HUB NATURAL GAS CONTINUOUS CONTRACT WITH COLUMN VOLUME BELOW

Chart 6-2 shows a zoomed section of the same Natural Gas chart. The columns being referred to below are numbered. X column 2 is 3 boxes shorter than O column 1, yet the volume is almost the same, showing the strength behind the X column and indicating that the buyers were not put off by the sharp fall in the previous column and have come back with a volume-backed move.

O column 3 has very low volume, as does O column 5. Notice that column 5 gave a double-bottom sell signal, but the low volume that accompanies it indicates caution should be taken when deciding whether to act on it. X column 4 has marginally higher volume than each of the O columns either side of it, even though there are fewer Xs in column 4 than in O column 5. Notice the increase in volume in X column 6, which gave a double-top buy signal. It could be argued that the volume is greater in column 6 because it's a longer column, but in fact Chart 6-3 – which shows the chart further back in time, before the final two Xs in column 6 have been added and prior to the double-top signal – shows that the volume was already high prior to the double-top signal and then increased further on and after the signal. The higher volume in X columns than O columns in this series is an indication that the pattern is gaining a bullish bias.

Referring again to Chart 6-2, O column 7 is the same length as X column 6, but the volume is much lower, showing that the selling volume to produce new Os is much lower than the buying volume to produce new Xs. The 3-box reversal in X column 8 is on low volume, which would normally have little significance, but notice that it managed to reverse a column of 8 Os on low volume, which shows that the commitment by the bears was not that strong. It took a small amount of volume to reverse by three Xs.

O column 9 then generates a triple-bottom sell, which would ordinarily be regarded as bearish, but notice that the volume was almost the lowest in the pattern, indicating that the signal should be treated with caution. The reason being that a triple-bottom break on low volume shows lack of commitment. In a case like this it is advisable to wait to see if the volume increases if further Os are printed. As you can see that did not happen, because before another O could be printed, X column 10 reversed into a double-top buy on high volume. Once again it may be argued that the volume is high because column 10 is a long column, but if you look at Chart 6-4 – which shows the chart further back in time, while column 10 was still being built and just after the double-top signal – you can see that the volume was already higher than the preceding O columns at the time of the double-top and went on to increase as the column continued building.

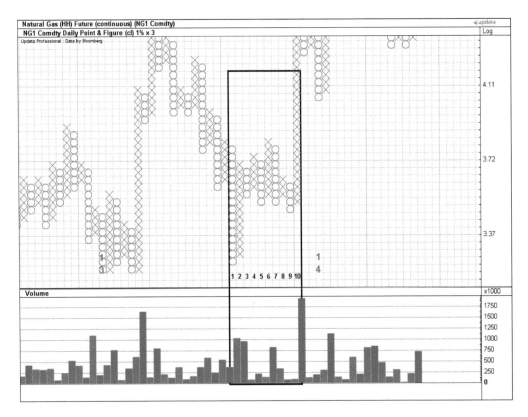

CHART 6-2: ZOOMED SECTION OF 1% X 3 HENRY HUB NATURAL GAS CONTINUOUS CONTRACT WITH COLUMN VOLUME BELOW

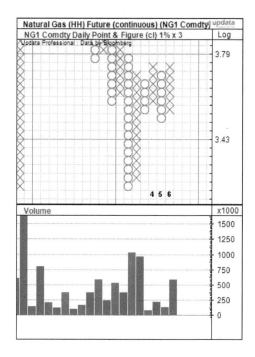

CHART 6-3: SHOWS THE VOLUME IN COLUMN 6 PRIOR TO THE DOUBLE-TOP SIGNAL

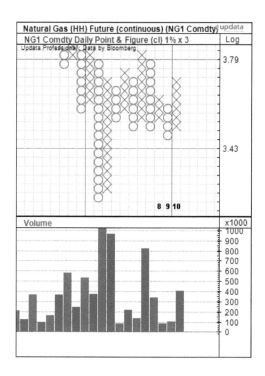

CHART 6-4: SHOWS THE VOLUME IN COLUMN 10 AFTER THE DOUBLE-TOP SIGNAL

Column volume may be used with any Point and Figure chart, including high/low, low/ high and ohlc constructed charts, 1-box reversal charts and those constructed with intraday interval history. With 1-box charts, it is possible, and not unusual, to have two or more up volume (blue) bars or down volume (red) bars next to one another. This occurs when there is a one-step back,[24] because a one-step back is merely a pause in the prevailing column rather than a reversal against it.

Chart 6-5 is a 1% x 1-box reversal chart of the Henry Hub Natural gas contract. The first thing to notice is the number of double blue and double red volume bars. These occur every time there is a one-step back in the Point and Figure chart. There is a triple blue up volume set of bars marked A on the chart showing three one-step backs, one after the other, as the price moved away from its historic 2012 low. The presence of these X column one-step backs shows strong demand, allowing a pull back of only one box before advancing again.

CHART 6-5: 1% X 1 HENRY HUB NATURAL GAS CONTINUOUS CONTRACT WITH COLUMN VOLUME BELOW

---

24 See page 6 for a description of one-step back.

Chart 6-6 is a 1% x 1 of Henry Hub Natural Gas showing the same zoomed section as that in the 3-box Chart 6-2. You can clearly see that blue X column volume bars are dominant in the pattern, giving it a bullish bias. The occurrence of double blue up volume bars, firstly as the price reacts from the low, marked A, and secondly as the price reacts back from the weak break of support, marked B, show the occurrence of one-step backs.

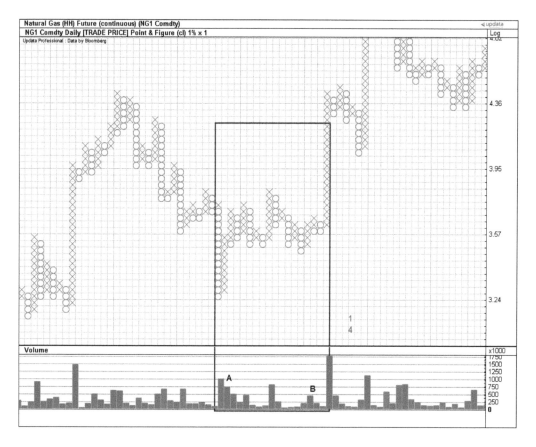

CHART 6-6: ZOOMED 1% X 1 HENRY HUB NATURAL GAS CONTINUOUS CONTRACT WITH COLUMN VOLUME BELOW

It is not necessary to show charts drawn with high/low construction or using interval data because they work in exactly the same way.

Although looking at each column and each volume bar gives you a lot of information about each column, a summary of it can effectively be generated by drawing an On-balance volume chart.

ON-BALANCE VOLUME (OBV)

On-balance volume (OBV), developed by Joseph Granville, is a cumulative line where, if the price change is positive the volume for the period is added to the cumulative line, and if it is negative it is subtracted. With Point and Figure charts, however, the column volume in X columns is added and that in O columns is subtracted from the cumulative line. It is in effect a summary of the inspection of each column volume and is therefore easier to read than the individual column volume bars.

This is demonstrated in Chart 6-7, which shows the same section of chart as that in Chart 6-2, but with the addition of an OBV chart. When discussing the column volume on pages 123-4, the conclusion was that the pattern in the highlighted section was bullish because the X column volumes were higher than the O column volumes. You can see that the OBV confirms this by trending up as the pattern is building, making the assessment of the pattern much easier. In fact, if you look at other patterns in the chart with the benefit of having the OBV chart, you can see how OBV can assist in the analysis of Point and Figure charts.

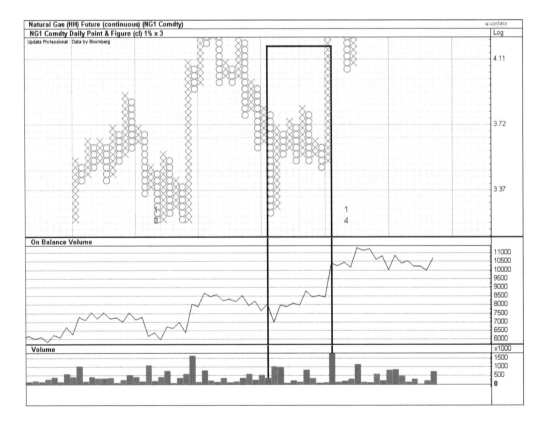

CHART 6-7: ZOOMED 1% X 3 HENRY HUB NATURAL GAS CONTINUOUS CONTRACT WITH ON-BALANCE VOLUME AND COLUMN VOLUME

To fully understand the impact of OBV, it is important to see what it looks like before the X column has broken out of the highlighted pattern in Chart 6-7 – in other words, what you would be seeing as the X column starts to build. Chart 6-8 shows the position earlier on in the column. Notice that the OBV has already broken out to a new high, even though the price is well below the highs.

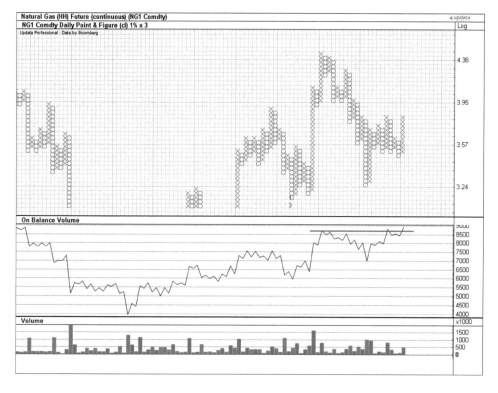

CHART 6-8: 1% X 3 HENRY HUB NATURAL GAS CONTINUOUS CONTRACT WITH ON-BALANCE VOLUME AND COLUMN VOLUME AT EARLIER DATE

OBV can be used with intraday interval charts in the same way, where instead of just one price per day to construct the Point and Figure chart there could be over 400 in the case of a 1 minute chart. You will recall that one of the advantages of using intraday data is that it allows you to use smaller box sizes, and in doing so gives you a shorter-term view.

Chart 6-9 is a 0.1% x 3 Point and Figure chart of Akamai Technologies Inc with an OBV chart below showing about 10 days' worth of 1 minute data. Notice that the X column marked A was accompanied by the sharp rise in the OBV, also marked A, showing enthusiastic accumulation. After a pullback of three Os, the price continued to rise, albeit on lower volume, as indicated by the OBV. It then declined sharply with the O column equally as long as the initial X column, however, the decline in OBV was small in comparison, indicating a lack of selling pressure. The price then continued to decline over a number of columns to point B, but once again the decline in the OBV was proportionally much smaller.

The price bottomed at point B and rose to a new high at point C, matched by a rising OBV, which also hit a new high at point C. At this stage everything looks good, but it's what happens next that is important. The price falls sharply to point D – this was on high volume, which you can see because the OBV fell sharply at the same time. The price then recovers to make a new high at point E, but look at the OBV – it does not match the new high, creating bearish divergence between points C and E. The occurrence of divergence is itself not a signal, but it is an alert that all is not well. The price then falls from point E, breaking the subjective trend line BD. It then rallies strongly to point F, but once again that price rise is not matched by a proportional move in the OBV, meaning that again there was low volume in the up move. From point F, the price and the OBV continue to decline together to the end of the chart.

Without adding OBV to your Point and Figure chart it would have been impossible to see that the chart started to become bearish after the unconfirmed high at point E which was followed by a break of the trend line.

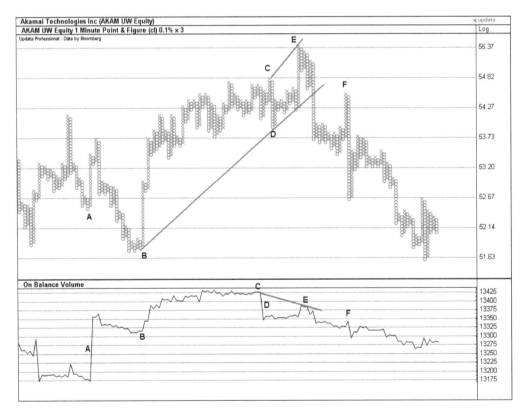

CHART 6-9: 0.1% X 3 CHART OF AKAMAI TECHNOLOGIES INC USING 1 MINUTE DATA WITH ON-BALANCE VOLUME BELOW

As stated earlier, OBV, when used with a Point and Figure chart, is a summary of the column volume because X column volume is added and O column volume is subtracted. Sometimes you will find that using OBV and column volume together adds even more to your analysis, as shown by Chart 6-8.

VOLUME-PRICE TREND (VPT)

Volume-Price Trend was developed by David Markstein in the early 1970s. It is also an accumulation/distribution line like OBV, but differs slightly in calculation. Whereas OBV adds or subtracts the column volume depending on whether it is an X column or O column, VPT ignores the direction of the column and instead multiplies the change in price from one column to the next by the volume of the next column. This brings a price element into volume analysis.

In Point and Figure terms this means multiplying the change in the midpoint column value (change in the 1 column moving average) by the volume. This has the effect of producing a much smoother line for VPT than the OBV. This is shown in Chart 6-10, which compares the OBV with VPT for Henry Hub Natural Gas.

CHART 6-10: 1% X 3 HENRY HUB NATURAL GAS CONTINUOUS CONTRACT WITH ON-BALANCE VOLUME AND VOLUME-PRICE TREND BELOW

Generally, the two lines show similar things. The interpretation is the same, so it's a matter of taste which one is used. However, you should note one thing: although you would expect a positive change when moving from an O column to an X column, or a negative change when moving from an X column to an O column, which is the case with OBV, it is possible to have the opposite effect with VPT. This is because the midpoint of an X column may actually be lower than the midpoint of the preceding O column, or the midpoint of an O column may be higher than the midpoint of the preceding X column, as shown by Chart 6-11.

Column A is an X column and column B is an O column. Since with OBV volume is added if X and subtracted if O, it falls from A to B. But notice that the midpoint of column B, the O column, is above the midpoint of the preceding X column marked A. This means the VPT rises rather than falls. So the large O column volume bar, marked B, causes OBV to fall, but the VPT to rise. In this particular case, although not always, VPT was a better measure of succeeding price action.

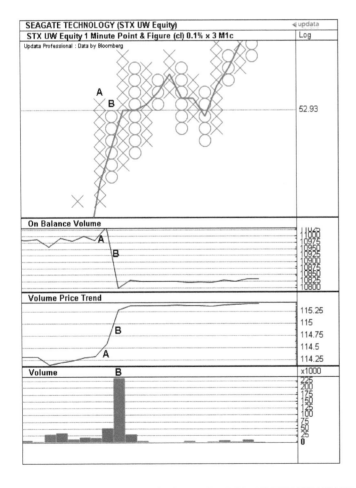

CHART 6-11: 1 MINUTE 0.1% X 3 OF SEAGATE TECHNOLOGY INC WITH OBV AND VPT

VOLUME AT PRICE

Although volume at price is another volume-based indicator, it is very different from the volume based charts discussed so far. It is a horizontal histogram created by adding up the volume at each box level (row) rather than for each column. As with column volume, only the volume that created each X or O is used in the summation. So if there are 15 Xs and Os across the chart at a particular price level, then the volumes that created those 15 Xs or Os are summed. It does not distinguish between Xs and Os. If either occurs at the price level, the volume behind it is summed looking back over the whole data history. Whereas column volume tells you the amount of volume used to build a column, volume at price tells you the amount of volume at any price level.

Volume at price tells you what the interest is at any price (box) level and whether it is significant by comparing the volumes at each level. The higher the volume at any level, the greater the activity and therefore the greater the interest and significance of the level. This high activity means that there is good two-way trade taking place at the level, with the buyers believing the price will go up and the sellers believing it will go down.

If the price falls from the high volume level, a large overhang of supply will exist at that level, which turns it into a resistance level to any up move, because the buyers who bought at that level will want to offload if it gets back to the level again and sellers who profited from their shorts will want another opportunity to sell. So, if after falling, the price rises and approaches the high volume resistance level again and breaks up through it, it means that the new demand is sufficiently strong to overcome the supply overhang at that level, which is bullish in nature.

Conversely, if the price rises from a high volume level, it creates a support level to any down move, because sellers caught on the wrong side of the market will want to close their shorts at the level and buyers will want another opportunity to buy having seen the price rise before. But if the price then falls back to the high volume level and breaks below it, it shows that any demand at that level has been taken up, which is considered bearish.

Chart 6-12 shows the position of the S&P 500 on 7 October 2002. The volume at price histogram shows the volume at each box level up to that date. There are three significant high volume areas, marked A, B and C. These show higher than normal volume, which may create resistance to any up move.

Chart 6-13 steps the chart forward to 30 January 2003. Notice how the high volume area A has provided resistance to the up move, showing that overhead supply existed at that level.

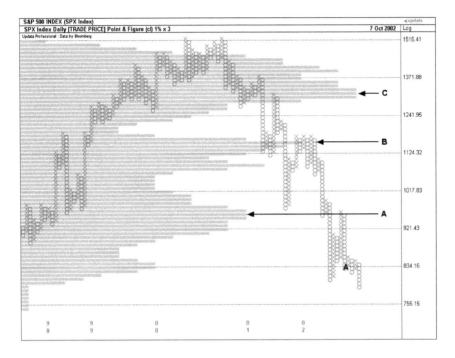

CHART 6-12: 1% X 3 OF S&P 500 AS AT 7 OCTOBER 2002 WITH VOLUME AT PRICE HISTOGRAM

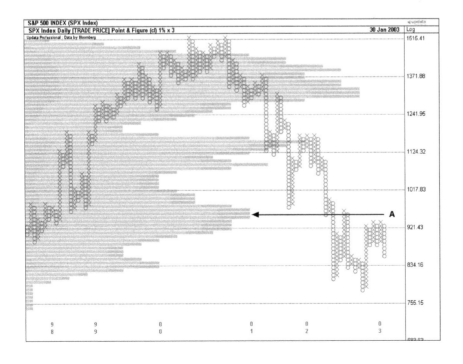

CHART 6-13: 1% X 3 OF S&P 500 AS AT 30 JANUARY 2003 WITH VOLUME AT PRICE HISTOGRAM

Chart 6-14 steps the chart forward to 4 October 2004. Notice, first, that once the price broke through the resistance of high volume area A, it moved sharply higher as buyers try to seek out sellers. It then encountered resistance at high volume area B where again overhead supply halted the advance.

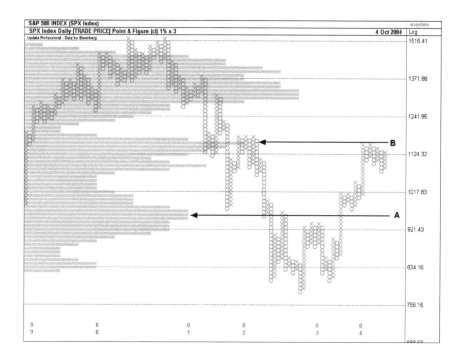

CHART 6-14: 1% X 3 OF S&P 500 AS AT 4 OCTOBER 2004 WITH VOLUME AT PRICE HISTOGRAM

Chart 6-15 shows the position as at 23 February 2007. Having overcome the resistance around area B, it advanced to area C, where it encountered resistance again, falling back for three columns before advancing strongly ahead. It is possible that area C provided less resistance than area B because the volume at that level occurred seven years previously and was possibly of less importance because any stale bulls may have already capitulated, leaving only the hardened few waiting for an opportunity to break even. It may have been that demand at that level was high and quickly took up any supply overhang and then had to track higher to find any sellers.

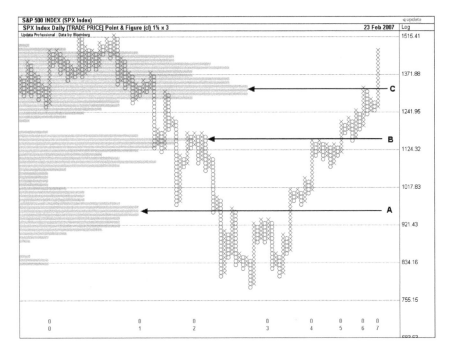

CHART 6-15: 1% X 3 OF S&P 500 AS AT 23 FEBRUARY 2007 WITH VOLUME AT PRICE HISTOGRAM

The important point to note about the support and resistance levels created by these high volume areas is that they can be broken. They may provide support or resistance for a time, but supply or demand will often lead to them being broken.

The clue to whether a support or resistance level will hold or be broken can be found by using column volume and OBV. Chart 6-16 takes the chart back to January 2006, as the price approaches the resistance level at C. Column volume and OBV are added to give more information. Notice that the volume in the last X column is higher than the last six X columns, causing OBV to break to a new high, higher even than in September 2000. The power behind the price as it approaches resistance indicates that the supply overhang at C is unlikely to fulfil the high demand, which is exactly what happened.

This discussion shows that you can't just use one indicator – you need a combination of indicators to help you make an assessment.

A note on price level activity

Closely associated with volume at price is price level activity, which counts the number of Xs and Os at any price level. Although volume is not a part of the calculation, the horizontal histogram looks similar. It is important that you understand the difference, which is explained under the heading 'Activity Histograms' in *The Definitive Guide to Point and Figure*.

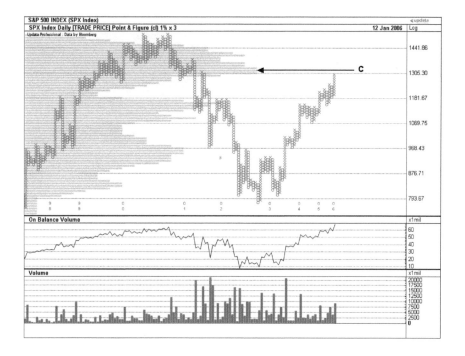

CHART 6-16: 1% X 3 OF S&P 500 AS AT 12 JANUARY 2006 WITH COLUMN VOLUME, OBV AND VOLUME AT PRICE HISTOGRAM

SUMMARY

Volume, once not a part of Point and Figure, is now an important component which aids the analysis of your Point and Figure chart. Knowing the volume behind building blocks in any column is vital for knowing the conviction behind the adding of those blocks. Patterns all look the same until the volume behind the columns in the pattern is added to the analysis to tell you whether the breakout has power behind it or not. Column volume therefore becomes essential when evaluating patterns.

Once the ability to calculate the volume in a column has been established, other volume indicators such as accumulation/distribution lines, On-balance volume and Volume-Price Trend can be used to great effect.

Because Point and Figure charts compartmentalise the data into boxes and because the volume that was behind the creation of the box is known, it is possible to measure volume horizontally. Volume at Price tells you the amount of interest there is at each box level, which in turn tells you where to expect support or resistance.

There are other volume-based indicators, such as positive and negative volume index, volume action, and many more. There is no reason why these can't be used with Point and Figure charts provided the Point and Figure chart is log scaled and the indicators are calculated using similar rules to the ones covered above.

Chapter Seven. New Point and Figure-Based Tools and Indicators

INTRODUCTION

ALL THE INDICATORS COVERED SO FAR ARE TIME-BASED INDICATORS modified for Point and Figure use. You will have seen that they enhance the Point and Figure chart and provide additional information which is not available from the plain Point and Figure chart. This section covers indicators and tools which do not exist outside Point and Figure charts, in that their calculations are imbedded in the Point and Figure chart itself.

The Point & Figure Trend Oscillator plots the difference between the price and 45° trend lines. Then, derived from Point and Figure's unique 45° trends is the ability to translate these on to time-based charts. Finally, the ability to show partial reversals to forewarn of a trend change is discussed.

POINT & FIGURE TREND OSCILLATOR

The Point & Figure Trend Oscillator[25] is a new indicator created to assess whether the Point and Figure chart is overbought or oversold using only Point and Figure methods as the basis for its calculation.

One of the advantages of 3-box reversal charts is that you can draw objective 45° trend lines which demarcate uptrends and downtrends. When the price breaks through a 45° line, another is drawn in the opposite direction, so trends oscillate between uptrend and downtrend. The Point & Figure Trend Oscillator measures the distance between the price and the 45° trend line, oscillating above and below a zero line.

In each case, the distance is measured from the 45° line to the last X in an X column and the last O in an O column. The distance can be measured in absolute (points) terms or in percentage terms. The parameters for the oscillator are the reversal and the box size, either a

---

25 The Point & Figure Trend Oscillator was devised by Jeremy du Plessis.

percentage box for an oscillator based on a log scale Point and Figure chart, or a points box based on an arithmetic Point and Figure chart. These parameters should match those used to draw the Point and Figure chart above the oscillator.

To calculate the oscillator, therefore, you must first draw a Point and Figure chart, then draw the main bullish and bearish 45° trend lines, which switch from bullish to bearish and vice versa every time the 45° trend is penetrated. Then calculate the number of points between the 45° line and the top of each X column or bottom of each O column. This may also be expressed as the percentage by which the top of each X column and the bottom of each O column is above or below the 45° line. It does not make any significant difference to the shape of th e indicator whether you use absolute or percentage differences in your calculation.

Because Point and Figure charts are on a squared grid, 45° trend lines show the rise or fall in price by the value of one box per column. So in a log scale 1% x 3 chart, the 45° line shows the rise or fall of 1% per column. A price maintaining this rise is therefore contained within the 45° uptrend; one maintaining this fall is contained within the 45° downtrend. The basis behind defining uptrends and downtrends with 45° lines is that if the price is unable to rise by the value of one box per column, it can no longer be considered to be in an uptrend and so it moves into a downtrend. Conversely, if it is not falling by more than the value of one box per column, it can no longer be in a downtrend and so moves into an uptrend. But prices often rise and fall by more than the value of one box per column, and in doing so, move away from the 45° line. The faster the rise or fall, the further the price moves away from the 45° line. The distance from the 45° line is measured by the Point & Figure Trend Oscillator and therefore you are measuring the extent to which the chart it is overbought or oversold.

If the price rises by the value of one box per column, the Point & Figure Trend Oscillator will plot sideways maintaining the same value because the distance between the price and the 45° line remains the same. A price rising to new highs, however, should increase the distance to the 45° line because it should be rising at more than the value of one box per column. If it does not and divergence occurs, it is a warning that the power behind the rise is decreasing. The same can happen if the falling price is not increasing the distance between it and the 45° line. The oscillator is really measuring the speed of any trend. The further it is away from zero, the greater the speed.

Chart 7-1 is a 1% x 3 of the Dow Jones Industrial Average going back to 1908,[26] with 45° trend lines in red, on which the Point & Figure Trend Oscillator plotted below it is based. In this example, because of the long history, the oscillator plots the percentage by which the price is above or below the 45° trend lines.

Notice that the price can become much more overbought than it can become oversold. The oscillator shows a maximum of 165% in 1929 compared to -70% in 1932. This of course is because the price can rise more than 100% above the 45° line but it can't fall more than 100% below it. This imbalance is common on indicators that have not been normalised, but

---

26   In order to fit the whole Point and Figure chart into the window, the Xs and Os have been reduced in size to the extent that it is not possible to distinguish between them.

does not affect the reading of them, because using key levels helps to see where the important turning points are.

As you can see, there are three levels of overbought and two of oversold. The upper overbought level at around 150% has been reached only twice in over 100 years – in 1929 and 1999 – which makes it a rare occurrence and so could be termed *super overbought*. Another level at around 80% has been reached many more times – in 1926, 1928, 1933, 1936, 1946, 1956, 1959, 1964 and 1987, as well as exceeded in 1929 and 1999. This can be regarded as the general overbought level and the more important one. At this level there is a distinct warning that a correction is due. You could also set a level, termed the *turnaround level*, at around the 40%, at which a number of turning points have occurred.

On the oversold side, the lower level at around -60% has only been reached once, in 1932. This level can be regarded a rare occurrence and the market can be considered as *super oversold*. The other level at around -20% is much more common, having been reached in 1915, 1917, 1921, 1938, 1941, 1970, 1974, 2002 and 2008/2009, and exceeded in 1932. At this level the market must be regarded as oversold and ready for a reversal.

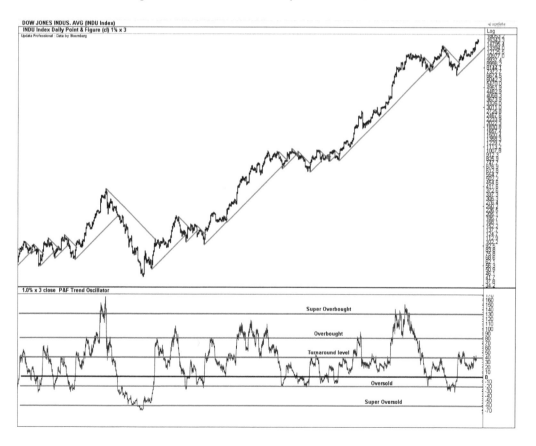

CHART 7-1: 1% X 3 OF THE DOW, WITH 1% X 3 POINT & FIGURE TREND OSCILLATOR

Divergence is an important part of reading any oscillator and the Point & Figure Trend Oscillator is no exception. As explained previously, divergence is not a signal, but rather a warning that the speed of the rise or fall is faltering. Moreover, divergence is not a prerequisite for a correction, so you can't assume that no divergence means there won't be a change in trend.

Chart 7-2 is a 1% x 3 of the S&P 500 with 45° trend lines drawn in red. Below is the 1% x 3 Point & Figure Trend Oscillator measuring the percentage that the price is above or below the 45° lines. Notice that divergence occurs at every major turning point.

Bullish divergence occurs when the price makes lower lows, but the Point & Figure Trend Oscillator makes higher lows shown by the blue lines below the action. Bearish divergence occurs when the price makes higher highs, but the Point & Figure Trend Oscillator makes lower highs, shown by the blue lines above the action.

You will recall that 45° trend lines are strengthened if the price comes back to touch the line after it has been drawn, as it did twice at point A. This means that when the Point & Figure Trend Oscillator bounces off the zero line, this can be regarded as bullish if the bounce is above the zero line, as it is at point A, or bearish if it is below.

You may question why the trend line touch at point B is not recorded as a bounce off zero on the Point & Figure Trend Oscillator. This is because at point B, the price is still under the influence of the 45° uptrend, which is only broken at point C, many columns after the touch of the downtrend line at point B. Only at the break of the uptrend at point C is the downtrend line drawn from the high. Of course the downtrend line could have been drawn earlier, whilst the uptrend was still in place, but the price can either be in an uptrend or a downtrend, not both.

45° trend lines were devised for use on 3-box reversal charts, but there is no reason why they and the Point & Figure Trend Oscillator can't be used to assist with the analysis of 1-box reversal charts. Because 1-box charts are flatter and the patterns wider, the 45° trends change often, as can be seen in Chart 7-3, which is a 1% x 1 of the S&P 500 with a Point & Figure Trend Oscillator based on 1-box rather than 3-box. In this example the oscillator is based on the absolute difference between the Point and Figure chart and the 45° trend lines. The oscillator shows overbought and oversold in the same way as it does with the 3-box version, as well as divergence at a number of the turning points. It gives a different perspective to the 3-box version, so it should not be ignored.

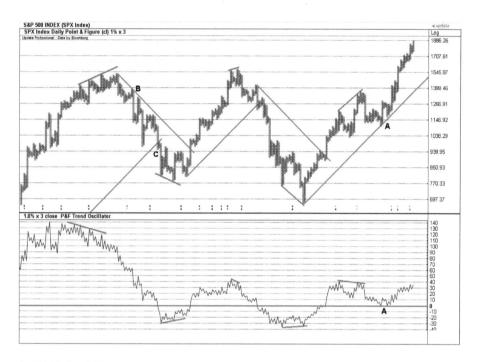

CHART 7-2: 1% X 3 OF THE S&P 500 WITH 1% X 3 POINT & FIGURE TREND OSCILLATOR SHOWING DIVERGENCE

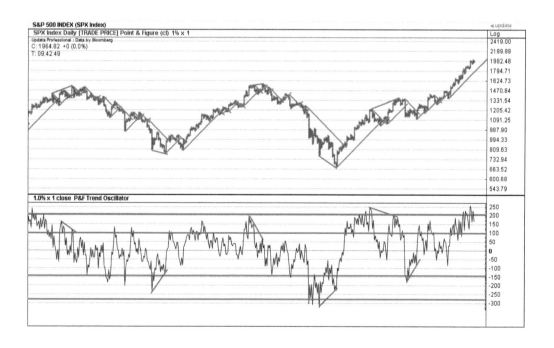

CHART 7-3: 1% X 1 OF THE S&P 500 WITH 1% X 1 POINT & FIGURE TREND OSCILLATOR

Chart 7-4 is an hourly 0.25% x 3 chart of gold with an absolute Point & Figure Trend Oscillator below. Notice how the oscillator flattens out as the lows in the price are made. Adding the oscillator helps you to assess when the 45° trend is reaching its extreme.

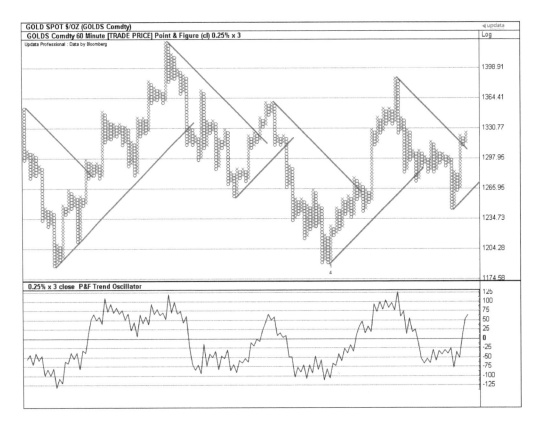

CHART 7-4: HOURLY 0.25% X 3 OF GOLD WITH 0.25% X 3 POINT & FIGURE TREND OSCILLATOR

POINT AND FIGURE'S GIFT TO TIME-BASED CHARTS

No one can deny the power of 45° lines, but those that don't or can't use Point and Figure are at a disadvantage. So, as a gift to them, two indicators that can be used on any time-based chart are presented below. For those who do use Point and Figure but don't use it exclusively, you will now be able to transfer these two Point and Figure indicators to your time-based charts. The first is the Point & Figure Trend Oscillator discussed above and the second is the translation of 45° trend lines directly on to a line or candle chart.

Point & Figure Trend Oscillator for time-based charts

Although the Point & Figure Trend Oscillator is constructed solely from a Point and Figure chart, it can be used with any time-based chart where a Point and Figure perspective is required. To do this, you must first draw a Point and Figure chart and add the 45° trend lines. Then for each X and O column, record the price level of the 45° line. Because columns can take a number of time periods to build, the price level of the 45° line applies to all the time periods within each column. For each time period on the time series chart, you therefore know the value of the 45° line as well as the price, so the Point & Figure Trend Oscillator is calculated measuring the absolute difference or percentage difference between the 45° level and the price for each period.

Chart 7-5 shows a line chart of the Dow Jones Industrial Average with the same Point & Figure Trend Oscillator that was used in Chart 7-1. This allows users of time-based charts to use a unique Point and Figure tool without having to display it with a Point and Figure chart.

CHART 7-5: LINE CHART OF THE DOW WITH 1% X 3 POINT & FIGURE TREND OSCILLATOR

The advantage of using the Point & Figure Trend Oscillator on time-based charts is that overbought and oversold is not measured by a time-based momentum oscillator, but by how far the Point and Figure chart is away from its 45° trend lines at any time. This means that although it is shown below a time-based chart, it is independent of any time-based influences.

The hourly chart of gold is shown here again, but this time as a line chart with the Point & Figure Trend Oscillator. Compare Chart 7-6 with the Point and Figure version used in Chart 7-4. The oscillator has the same value at any given time but does not plot identically, because the x-axis spacing is different, but both show similar areas of overbought and oversold.

CHART 7-6: HOURLY LINE CHART OF GOLD WITH 0.25% X 3 POINT & FIGURE TREND OSCILLATOR

45° trend lines on time-based charts

It is common knowledge that it is impossible to draw consistent 45° lines on time-based charts, because the angle changes as the aspect ratio of the chart changes and the lines then pass through different points on the chart. Because the aspect of a Point and Figure chart is constant, being based on a squared grid, true 45° lines are possible and these have historically been a powerful analysis tool available only to Point and Figure analysts. Not any more: it is possible to translate Point and Figure 45° lines on to your time-based charts by simply providing the parameters required, just as you would when using the Point & Figure Trend Oscillator on time-based charts. Once again, it is important to remember when doing this that columns can take more than one time period to build, but the level of the 45° trend line is constant for each column. So to translate 45° trend lines on to time-based charts, you take the start date and end date of each column and plot the same level that the 45° trend line is at for all those periods.

Chart 7-7 is 0.5% x 3 Point and Figure chart of the euro with standard 45° trend lines, marking out the changes in trend. Chart 7-8 is a line chart of the euro with the same 45° trend lines translated on to it. The trend lines are not straight lines on the line chart because the x-axis spacing is different from the x-axis on the Point and Figure chart, but they mark out exactly where the 45° trend lines are on the y-axis. The flat sections are due to the fact that X and O columns can take a number of days to build, but during that time, the value of the 45° line is the same.

It is, however, important to note that although the Point and Figure chart is constructed using the close price, the last X and last O in any column will not be the actual close price recorded on the line chart, because the line chart price may not be sufficient to fill the next Point and Figure box. For this reason, the 45° lines, which are based on X column highs and O column lows, may be penetrated slightly by the close line chart, but these penetrations don't result in a change in trend.

This occurred twice on line Chart 7-8 and is marked by points A and B, which are also marked on Point and Figure Chart 7-7. For the same reason, the point marked C in Chart 7-8 looks like the line is on the 45° trend when in fact it is two boxes away on the Point and Figure chart. This should not concern you. Only genuine breaks of the 45° line on the Point and Figure chart will change its direction on the line chart.

CHART 7-7: 0.5% X 3 OF THE EURO WITH 45° TREND LINES

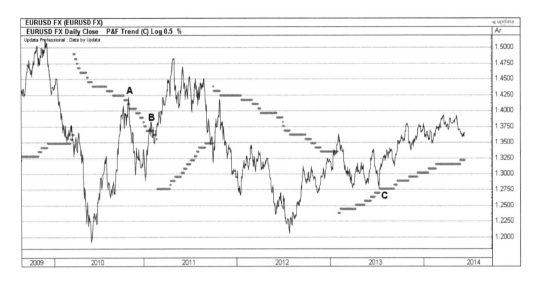

CHART 7-8: LINE CHART OF THE EURO WITH POINT AND FIGURE 45° TREND LINES TRANSLATED FROM A 1% X 3 POINT AND FIGURE CHART

So that you can compare the different ways of using and drawing 45° trends, Chart 7-9 is an hourly line chart of gold with 0.25% x 3 45° trend lines translated on to it. Compare this chart with Chart 7-4, which is a 0.25% x 3 Point and Figure chart with 45° trend lines and Point & Figure Trend Oscillator, and Chart 7-6, which is a line chart with a 0.25% x 3 Point & Figure Trend Oscillator. All lines are derived from the 45° trend lines on a 0.25% x 3 Point and Figure chart.

If you prefer working with bar or candle charts, then the 45° trend lines should be translated from a Point and Figure chart constructed using the high/low or low/high construction method instead of the close only, as used in the earlier charts. This is because the highs and lows of the X and O columns will be based on price highs and lows, as will the 45° lines.

CHART 7-9: HOURLY LINE CHART OF GOLD WITH 45° TREND LINES TRANSLATED FROM A 0.25% X 3 POINT AND FIGURE CHART

Chart 7-10 is a bar chart of the euro with 45° trend lines translated from a 1% x 3 high/low constructed Point and Figure chart of the euro. In order to show where the Point and Figure chart crosses the 45° lines, vertical lines have been added to the translated trend lines on the bar chart. For comparison, Chart 7-11 is the 1% x 3 high/low constructed Point and Figure chart of the euro with 45° lines showing the same section of data so you can see how the translation works.

No time-based lines can replicate this trend analysis and so this is an addition to the range of tools that can be used on time-based charts.

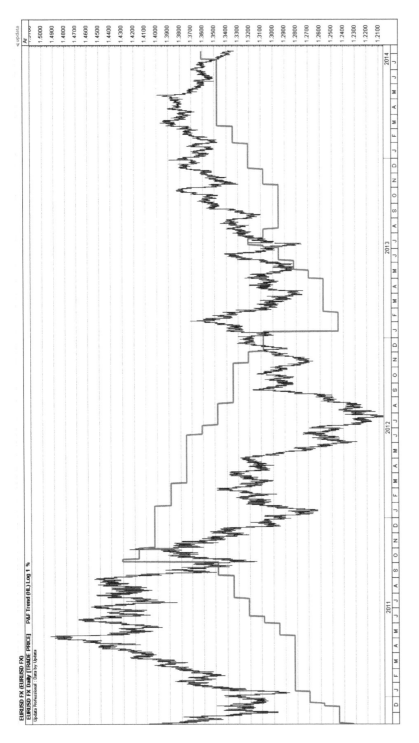

CHART 7-10: BAR CHART OF THE EURO WITH POINT AND FIGURE 45° TREND LINES TRANSLATED FROM A 1% X 3 HIGH/LOW CONSTRUCTED POINT AND FIGURE CHART

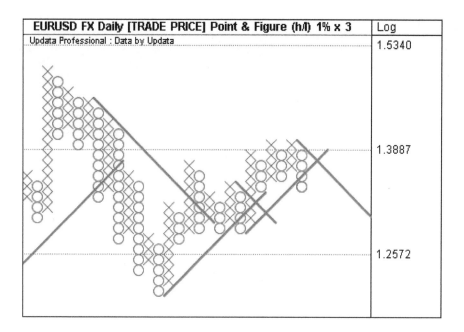

CHART 7-11: 1% X 3 HIGH/LOW CONSTRUCTED POINT AND FIGURE CHART OF THE EURO WITH 45° TREND LINES

Even 45° trends from very short-term charts can be translated on to time-based charts. Chart 7-12 is a 1 minute chart of the soybeans future with 0.05% 45° Point and Figure trend lines translated on to the line chart. Notice how in line chart form, what were straight 45° lines on a Point and Figure chart curve around the price on the line chart and objectively define the trends.

CHART 7-12: HOURLY LINE CHART OF SOYBEANS FUTURE WITH POINT AND FIGURE 45° LINES

POINT AND FIGURE REVERSAL ALERT

The Point and Figure reversal alert is not an indicator, but another way to display the charts. It's another 21st century improvement in Point and Figure chart display. One of the problems with Point and Figure charts, especially 3-box reversal upwards, is that you are not alerted to a possible column change (a reversal) until it happens. Some will argue that this is exactly what Point and Figure charts are all about and that no alert is required, and they are right.

To obtain alerts, a lot of short-term traders use 2-box reversal charts, which change columns sooner. Whichever camp you are in, it is sensible to use two different box sizes because the smaller box size alerts you to the fact that the larger box size chart may be about to reverse.

The Point and Figure reversal alert goes some way to answering the problem of the hidden partial reversal. This is done by adding a new column to the chart, and instead of placing an X or O, simply shading it so you can see immediately what the current price position is and whether there is a possible reversal.

Chart 7-13 shows the top in gold. After a strong move up, gold made a high in August 2011, but then corrected back for a month. In September it broke to a new high again, but for that break to be valid, it should continue to rise with no pause. However, after a break of only one box, the price retraced back by 2 boxes, or $20, to below the August high, as shown by the red shaded boxes in the last column. This is an incomplete reversal, alerting you to the possibility of a full reversal occurring. A normal Point and Figure chart would not have shown anything until the price reversed by 3 boxes, without warning, indicating that the break to the new high had failed.

The filtering of noise by waiting for a 3-box reversal is what Point and Figure charts are designed to do and showing the partial reversals removes that filter. However, remember that the partial reversals are not permanent columns on the Point and Figure chart. If in this example the price continued higher, the red shaded section would be removed, so shading does not alter the construction of the Point and Figure chart.

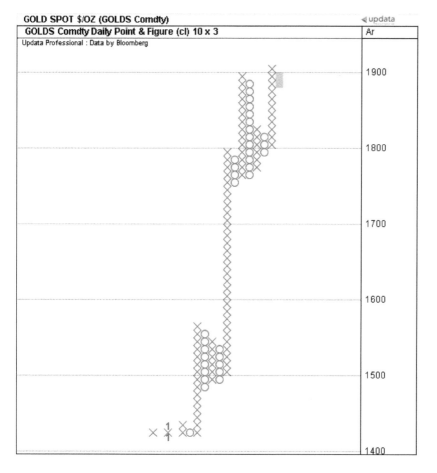

CHART 7-13: 10 X 3 OF GOLD SHOWING A PARTIAL REVERSAL

SUMMARY

This chapter has introduced indicators that have their origin in Point and Figure – they are not time-based indicators adapted to work with Point and Figure. Point and Figure analysts know that 45° lines on Point and Figure charts describe trends objectively, so an overbought/oversold oscillator created from these lines becomes a powerful tool. Because it measures the distance between the price and the 45° trend lines, it tells you whether the price is extended and whether it is no longer rising at one box per reversal (which is what a 45° trend line shows).

Analysts of time-based charts have looked on in envy at the ability of Point and Figure analysts to draw 45° lines on their Point and Figure charts, but it is possible now to translate Point and Figure 45° lines on to time-based charts, using the Point and Figure parameters to construct the lines. These 45° trends are not straight lines on time-based charts for obvious reasons, but they seem to mimic the shape of a trailing stoploss, which is essentially what they are. The fact that 45° trend lines can be translated from Point and Figure to time-based charts has meant that the Point & Figure Trend Oscillator can also be used. This allows candle and line charts to benefit from an oscillator that is not a traditional time-based oscillator.

Finally, although not an indicator but rather an appearance enhancement, partial reversals may be shown on Point and Figure charts to avoid the need to use smaller box sizes to pre-empt a breakout.

Chapter Eight. Advanced Analysis of Relative Strength and Spreads

DRAWING RELATIVE STRENGTH CHARTS AS POINT AND FIGURE charts enhances the analysis of them. The techniques explored so far in this book have all been with Point and Figure charts of price, so this chapter is dedicated to applying these advanced techniques to relative strength and spreads.

Relative strength[27] is used mainly in the equity markets and is a ratio chart of the stock to its index. A rising relative strength chart shows the stock is performing better than the index and a falling chart shows it is performing worse.

Spreads are used mainly in the commodity markets and are the difference between two related commodities or two contracts of the same commodity. Although these also measure relative performance their main purpose is to exploit the differences in price. No matter how they are used, the analysis is the same.

RELATIVE STRENGTH

The Definitive Guide to Point and Figure described how you can apply 45° trend lines to relative strength to help you to objectively decide the trend. In addition, Point and Figure targets can be used to get some idea about the potential of the relative strength chart. Now, with the information gained in the earlier chapters in this book, you may also use other tools such as oscillators with relative strength charts.

A note about relative strength scaling

Since relative strength charts are usually read in conjunction with the stock's price chart, it is important, when using Point and Figure, that they have the same time horizon. This is not an issue with time-based charts, but with Point and Figure the box size determines the time horizon, so the relative strength chart and the price chart must use the same box size. The only way to ensure this is to use the same percentage box size to draw log scale charts of

---

27 Relative Strength is in no way related to the similarly named Relative Strength Index (RSI), discussed in Chapter 5.

both price and relative strength. If your price chart is 1% x 3, therefore, your relative strength chart should also be 1% x 3.

Relative strength is the result of the price divided by the index, which means it is just a number which, depending on the stock price, can be very large or very small, making it impossible to glean any information from the scale and impossible to compare one relative strength chart to another.

The Definitive Guide to Point and Figure introduced a normalised scale for relative strength charts which makes the charts much more readable. To do this, you decide on a base date, the beginning of the year for example, then you divide each period's relative strength value by the relative strength value on the base date, then multiply by 100. This gives you a scale which is whole numbers and which immediately tells you the extent to which the stock has outperformed or underperformed the index, allowing you to compare relative strength charts of the stocks in your universe. A normalised relative strength value of 123 means that the stock has outperformed the benchmark index by 23%, whereas a value of 74 means it has underperformed by 26%.

Using advanced techniques on relative strength

Chart 8-1 is a 1% x 3 normalised relative strength chart of IBM Corp. relative to the S&P 500. The first thing to notice is the scaling. The current relative strength value is 70.09, which means that IBM has underperformed the S&P 500 by 29.91% since 2 January 2013. This not only allows you to see the state of IBM relative to the index, but it also allows you to compare and rank IBM with other stocks in the S&P 500.

The second thing to notice is how clearly the trends are defined by the 45° trend lines, making it easy to determine the relative strength trend. Finally, the vertical and horizontal targets give you some idea of the potential moves in the relative strength.

It is not just 45° trend lines that can be used – the Parabolic SAR used in conjunction with double-top and double-bottom signals is also an effective method for determining the relative strength trend.

Chart 8-2 is the same 1% x 3 normalised relative strength chart of IBM Corp. relative to the S&P 500, but this time with a 0.02 Parabolic SAR. The buy and sell signals are generated by Point and Figure signals after the price has crossed the Parabolic. Notice that at point A, although the price penetrated the Parabolic, there was no subsequent double-bottom sell.

CHART 8-1: 1% X 3 NORMALISED RELATIVE STRENGTH CHART OF IBM CORP. VS S&P 500

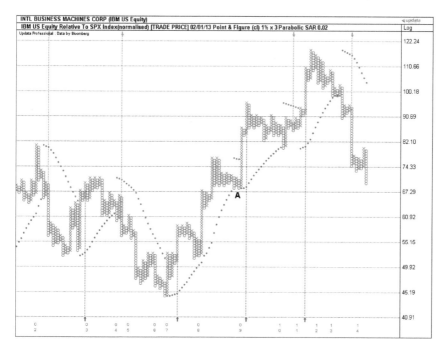

CHART 8-2: 1% X 3 NORMALISED RELATIVE STRENGTH CHART OF IBM CORP. VS S&P 500 WITH A 0.02 PARABOLIC SAR

Although exposing the trend objectively and establishing targets enhances relative strength analysis, the targets don't tell you whether the relative strength chart is extended (overbought or oversold) or not. As with price Point and Figure charts, you may add oscillators to assist with that analysis.

Chart 8-3 is a 1% x 3 relative strength chart of IBM Corp. again, with a 7 column RSI of the relative strength Point and Figure chart. Immediately you are provided with more information about the state of the relative strength chart.

You can see that when it reached a high at point C, it was also recording overbought, above 70, on the RSI and a correction followed. When the relative strength made a higher high at point D, not only was it above 70 again on the RSI, but the RSI showed divergence, which was a warning that the relative strength was running out of momentum.

Divergence is also shown when the relative strength reached a low at point A and a lower low at point B, not matched by a lower low on the RSI, which was rising from an oversold level below 30. Notice that the relative strength reached a low at point E with the RSI very oversold below 30. The relative strength went on to fall further but the RSI has not matched the lower action, although this can't be termed divergence until the RSI makes a second higher low.

CHART 8-3: 1% X 3 NORMALISED RELATIVE STRENGTH CHART OF IBM CORP. VS S&P 500 WITH 7 COLUMN RSI SHOWING DIVERGENCE

The analysis is not limited to adding oscillators. Chart 8-4 is a 2% x 3 relative strength chart of American Express against the S&P 500, with 10 column Bollinger bands and a 26,12 column MACD. Notice the squeeze circled, which coincided with a turn of the MACD. The MACD helps you to work out what direction the relative strength will take after the squeeze.

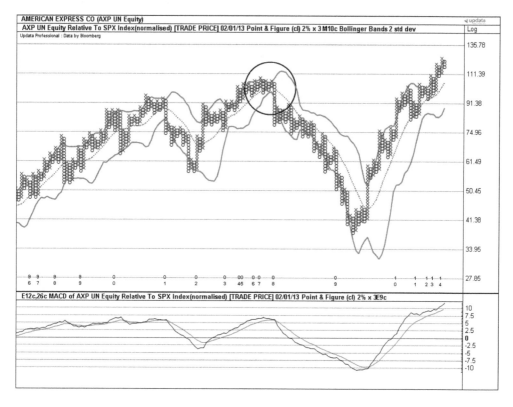

CHART 8-4: 2% X 3 NORMALISED RELATIVE STRENGTH CHART OF AMERICAN EXPRESS CO. VS S&P 500 WITH 26,12C MACD

Although only a small selection have been shown, any tool and any indicator used for the analysis of Point and Figure of price can be used to analyse relative strength Point and Figure charts.

SPREADS

A *spread* is the difference between two equities, two indices, two commodities or two contracts of the same commodity. Although spreads often oscillate above and below a zero line, it is still possible to draw a Point and Figure chart of the spread and use all the tools now available, including targets. There is, however, a big difference in scaling. Spreads can be negative so it is impossible to draw a log scaled chart of a spread using percentage box sizes, because it is not possible to take the log of a negative number. This means the box sizes in spreads are always arithmetic.

In any case, spreads tend to be analysed independently from the price of any of the components, so there is no need to match the spread box size with the box size of the price. Furthermore, it is not necessary to adjust the scale as it is with relative strength, because the raw value of the spread is important, as it tells you the difference in price between two instruments.

Using advanced techniques on spreads

The advantages of analysing spreads as Point and Figure charts are obvious and the same as those for analysing price and relative strength; exactly the same tools and charts may be used. Chart 8-5 is a 1 minute 0.25 x 3 of the December 14 live cattle-corn spread with 45° trend lines and vertical targets, with a 26,12 column MACD below. The targets have proved accurate in the past and are pointing to an even higher spread value of around -273, but notice that the MACD has rolled over, indicating a pause, if not a correction. A number of 45° internals have been broken, showing a weakening of the uptrend. Without these tools, analysing a bare spread chart is much more difficult.

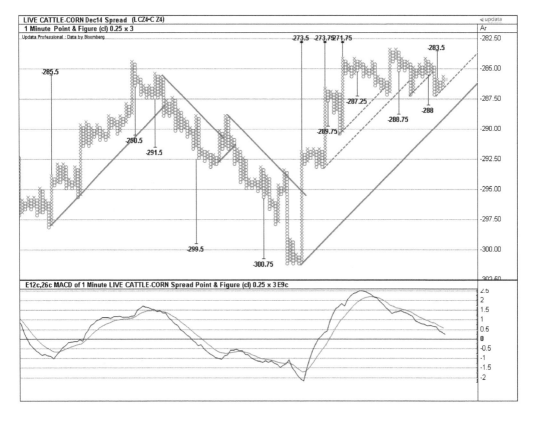

CHART 8-5: 0.25 X 3 DECEMBER 14 LIVE CATTLE-CORN SPREAD WITH 45° TREND LINES AND TARGETS AND 26,12 MACD

Chart 8-6 is a 0.5 x 3 Point and Figure chart of the ICE WTI-Brent spread based on 30 minute data, with a 10 column moving average and 26,12 column MACD. Note that the double-top and double-bottom signals after the moving average crossover coincide with the important turns in the MACD and signal line crossovers, with the exception of the whipsaw buy and sell signals circled. When the buy in the circled area was signalled, the signal line did not cross the MACD and although it crossed a few columns later, the sell signal had been generated and the spread continued to fall. So the simple addition of the MACD could have helped you to avoid a bad signal.

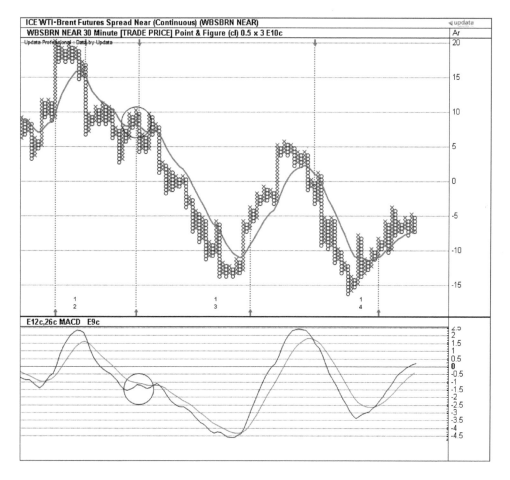

CHART 8-6: 0.5 X 3 WTI-BRENT CRUDE OIL SPREAD WITH 10 COLUMN MOVING AVERAGE AND 26,12 MACD

Even the use of Donchian channels can enhance the analysis of spreads. Chart 8-7 is a 0.5 x 3 of the Nymex 3-2-1 Crack spread with 5 column Donchian channels. Sell signals are marked A, C and E; buy signals are marked B and D. A buy alert marker has been placed at F but has not been exceeded.

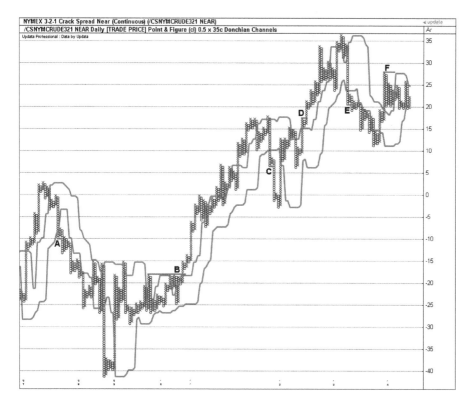

CHART 8-7: 0.5 X 3 NYMEX 3-2-1 CRACK SPREAD WITH 5 COLUMN DONCHIAN CHANNELS

Although the example charts have all been of commodities, the analysis is no different if the spreads are equities, indices or any other instrument.

SUMMARY

Most who use relative strength use it in its raw form of one price divided by another, but normalising relative strength makes the scale meaningful without changing the shape of the chart. It allows you to see how a stock has performed in percentage terms against the index, but more importantly allows you to compare the relative strength of one stock to another, allowing you to rank them, something that is not possible with relative strength in its raw form.

It is clear that using Point and Figure for the analysis of relative strength and spreads has always had advantages. Targets may be obtained allowing you to get some idea of how far the relative strength or spread will go.

The use of objective 45° trend lines has allowed the trend analysis of relative strength and spreads to become more objective. You have seen that the use of moving averages, Bollinger bands, Parabolic and Donchian channels have added more power to the analysis of these derivative charts, but it is the addition of indicators such as MACD, RSI and others calculated from the relative strength and spread Point and Figure charts that allow the analyst to assess relative strength and spreads with more confidence.

Chapter Nine. 21st Century Market Breadth

MARKET BREADTH INDICATORS ACCUMULATE THE NUMBER, OR measure the percentage, of stocks in a universe (usually an index), that fulfil some condition. The condition could be anything from the number of advances less declines, to the percentage of stocks hitting new highs, or something like the percentage of stocks with an RSI value above 50. There are literally hundreds of different breadth measures. If you are unfamiliar with the concept of market breadth, you are urged to read up on it.

It is important when calculating these market breadth indicators that the index of stocks is large and does not have regular reviews. Some capitalisation indices have their constituents reviewed every three months and at these times the laggards are removed and replaced by leaders. This gives a false market breadth reading because it is biased towards the bullish side.

ANALYSING PERCENTAGE MARKET BREADTH CHARTS

A full analysis of Point and Figure-based market breadth charts is undertaken in *The Definitive Guide to Point and Figure*, so this is just a brief description of what they mean and what to look for.

Point and Figure market breadth charts are based on the percentage of stocks fulfilling some Point and Figure condition so they all have a fixed scale of 0 to 100. They are effectively overbought/oversold indicators based on all the constituents of an index, not on the index itself, and hence the name 'breadth'. Above 70% is considered overbought, with anything below 30% considered oversold. The 50% level separates bull market from bear.

Dips below 30% are good opportunities to start looking for stocks in the universe giving Point and Figure buy signals. It is almost like someone has fired the starting gun. This is the very early stage of a new bull market where certain stocks lead. The first confirmation comes when the indicator rises above 30%, meaning that more stocks are starting to turn bullish. The second confirmation comes when the breadth indicator crosses up through the 50% level, signalling there is no longer any uncertainty and a new bull market has started. A move above 70% confirms that every stock barring the remaining 30% is bullish. It is usual for the indicator to oscillate above the 50% and around the 70% level while stock rotation takes place. Those that performed early on in the run are sold and replaced by those giving new buy signals.

Market breadth indicators based on Point and Figure are traditionally drawn as Point and Figure charts, which allows Point and Figure analysis of the breadth chart, but they can and should also be drawn as line charts, because this allows turning points to be lined up with the index itself and divergence can be assessed. You will be familiar with the concept of divergence and this also plays a part in the analysis of market breadth charts. This occurs when the index hits new highs or lows and the breadth indicator does not.

20TH CENTURY MARKET BREADTH

Point and Figure made a contribution to the library of market breadth indicators over 60 years ago, when a breadth indicator called Bullish Percent was devised by A.W. Cohen. It measures the percentage of stocks in a universe where the last signal was a double-top buy, on the assumption bullishness is measured by the last Point and Figure signal.

This means that Bullish Percent must be based on 3-box reversal stock charts so there is no ambiguity with the signals. To calculate the indicator, you must first draw a Point and Figure chart of every individual stock, then count the number where the last signal was a double-top buy, and then work out what percentage of the universe this represents.

Although Bullish Percent is a 20th century market breadth indicator, it is covered here in order that you have something with which to compare the two new Point and Figure breadth indicators, X-Column Percent and Bullish Trend Percent.

Chart 9-1 shows the S&P 500 with a 2% Bullish Percent of its constituents. This means that each stock chart has a box size of 2% and 3-box reversal when they are assessed. Familiarise yourself with the chart as it will be referred to when discussing the two new breadth indicators. In order to aid the comparison, a line chart is used rather than the traditional Point and Figure chart of the Bullish Percent so that the time scale can be seen and turning points compared.

One of the criticisms levelled at Bullish Percent is that it accumulates stocks where the last signal was a double-top buy, but because reversing from a double-top buy to a double-bottom sell requires a minimum reversal of five Os, it takes considerable negative price action to turn the stock chart bearish. Figure 9-1 shows why that is the case. A double-top buy occurs in column 3, adding the stock to the Bullish Percent count. Even if the breakout is only one X as it is in column 3, five Os are required in column 4 to reverse the double-top into a double-bottom, removing it from a bullish percent count.

CHART 9-1: LINE CHART OF THE S&P 500 WITH 2% BULLISH PERCENT OF THE S&P 500 MEMBERS

FIGURE 9-1: SHOWING THE NUMBER OF OS REQUIRED TO REVERSE A DOUBLE-TOP BUY INTO A DOUBLE-BOTTOM SELL

In Chart 9-1, Bullish Percent is based on 2% stock charts, which means the price must fall by at least 10% (five boxes) in order to reverse the double-top buy into a double-bottom sell. This means you may be counting stocks which have already turned bearish on other criteria, but have not yet given the double-bottom sell. If this is seen as a problem, the solution is to base Bullish Percent on a smaller percentage box size, say 1% or even 0.5%, which will give a shorter-term view.

21st CENTURY MARKET BREADTH

Market breadth is no exception to the considerable changes that are taking place with Point and Figure in the 21st century. Two new indicators are introduced here – X-Column Percent and Bullish Trend Percent – which give a shorter and longer-term view respectively.

X-Column Percent

X-Column[28] Percent measures the percentage of stocks in a universe that are currently in an X column and that means those that are in an intermediate uptrend. As with Bullish Percent, it is based on 3-box reversal charts. By definition, it is not as onerous to switch from bullish to bearish as it is with Bullish Percent described above, because it requires a reversal of only three boxes to switch from an O column to an X column and vice versa. Consequently, therefore, X-Column Percent is a shorter-term breadth indicator and should be used for short-term timing. What this means is that X-Column Percent can give you repeat entry points during a bull market already signalled by Bullish Percent.

Remaining with the line chart version for ease of comparison, Chart 9-2 shows the S&P 500 with a 2% X-Column Percent of its constituents. You can see immediately that X-Column Percent is a much shorter-term chart, as shown by the increased volatility, but take a ruler and line up the many lows in the indicator with the index itself and you will see that they line up with lows in the index. Penetrations of the 30% level are excellent buying opportunities of not only the constituents but of the index itself. Remember that the indicator is not calculated off the S&P 500, but rather off each stock in the index.

---

28 X-Column Percent was introduced for the first time in the second edition of *The Definitive Guide to Point and Figure*.

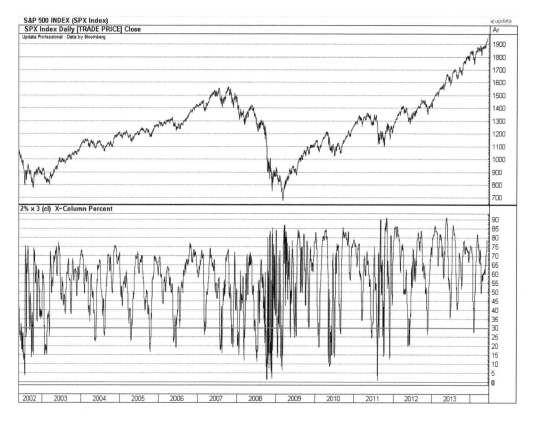

CHART 9-2: LINE CHART OF THE S&P 500 WITH 2% X-COLUMN PERCENT OF THE S&P 500 MEMBERS

Normally you would not show 12 years of history on a short-term indicator, so Chart 9-3 shows 2 years. Compare this with Bullish Percent Chart 9-1 and notice that Bullish Percent signalled the start of a new bull trend in August 2011 when it dipped below 30%, but it has not done so again, so if you missed that signal it would have been difficult to know when other opportunities existed. These are shown in Chart 9-3 when X-Column Percent dips below the 30% level. Remember the 50% level is important and it is the line that separates short-term uptrends from short-term downtrends.

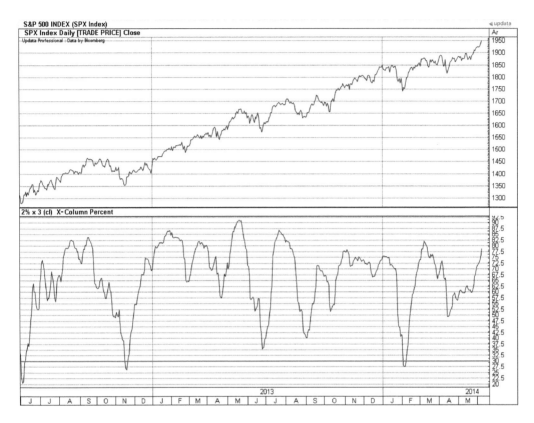

CHART 9-3: ZOOMED LINE CHART OF THE S&P 500 WITH 2% X-COLUMN PERCENT OF THE S&P 500 MEMBERS

Bullish Trend Percent

You have seen that Point and Figure 45° lines play an important part in Point and Figure analysis and define whether the chart is in a bull or bear trend. Bullish Trend Percent[29] measures the percentage of stocks in the universe that are above the 45° bullish support line – in other words, those that are in an uptrend. Once again it must be calculated off 3-box reversal stock charts.

Bullish Trend Percent ranks as the longest term of the three Point and Figure breadth indicators because changes in 45° trend take place less often than switches from double-top buys to double-bottom sells, or from O columns to X columns.

Chart 9-4 shows the S&P 500 with 2% Bullish Trend Percent below. The parameters are kept constant to allow direct comparison between the three market breadth indicators. In 12 years, there has only been one dip below 30% and that occurred over the period from the

---

29   Bullish Trend Percent was introduced for the first time in the second edition of *The Definitive Guide to Point and Figure*.

end of 2008 to the beginning of 2009, with the break back above 30 occurring in April 2009. Soon after it crossed through 50%, signalling a new long-term bull market, and has remained above ever since. So Bullish Trend Percent is a longer-term indicator than Bullish Percent.

CHART 9-4: LINE CHART OF THE S&P 500 WITH 2% BULLISH TREND PERCENT OF THE S&P 500 MEMBERS

USING BREADTH INDICATORS TOGETHER

Having three market breadth indicators based on Point and Figure makes the analysis of breadth much easier because each indicator has a different time horizon, all other things being equal. Bullish Trend Percent tells you when everything is in place for a new secular bull market to start. Bullish Percent identifies the primary trends within the secular bull and X-Column Percent identifies secondary trends within the primary trends.

Once Bullish Trend Percent has signalled the start of a secular bull market, as it did in 2008/2009, its work is done until at the end of the secular bear market and it falls below 30 again. You can then use Bullish Percent to help you to get the timing of your move back into the market right by identifying the start of primary bull trends within the secular bull. Doing so will give you additional entry points, as it did in 2010 and 2011. Within those primary bull trends there are secondary trends identified by X-Column Percent. These give you additional short-term entry points, as in June 2012, November 2012, July 2013 and February 2014.

It is important to remember that market breadth indicators are not designed to analyse the underlying index; their purpose is to switch you into bullish or bearish mode to tell you to start looking at the stocks that make up the index in order to find opportunities to buy or sell. That said, you will notice that X-Column Percent picks the turning points in the index very effectively and may be used to do that. Market Breadth indicators are better at marking out lows and times to buy than highs and times to sell. When these indicators are above 70 it does not mean sell all your holdings, but rather you should look to rotate out of stocks that have performed and into those that have not.

ADJUSTING YOUR TIME HORIZON

The time horizon of all Point and Figure-based market breadth indicators can be varied by adjusting the box size used to calculate the breadth. In the examples above, a box size of 2% was used, which means the Point and Figure chart for every stock in the index was drawn as 2% x 3 to assess its bullishness. 2% is a fairly long-term time horizon, so you can shorten it by choosing a box size of 1% or even 0.5%, but you can't keep reducing the box size maintaining daily time-series data. At some stage you have to switch to intraday interval data. This allows much smaller box sizes, which shorten the time horizon even further.

Consider, for example, Bullish Trend Percent. With daily charts, trends only change every few years, but on 1 minute data with a small box size, they could change every few hours, days or weeks. This means you can fine tune your entry points by calculating market breadth on intraday data with a small box size.

Chart 9-5 is a 1 minute chart of the S&P 500 with a Bullish Trend Percent calculated off 1 minute data of the constituents with a 0.1% box size. The chart is more volatile because the 45° trends change more often with 1 minute data, but once again dips below 30 are good opportunities to move into the market short term. Notice too that the indicator moves into the 90 area at tops in the index.

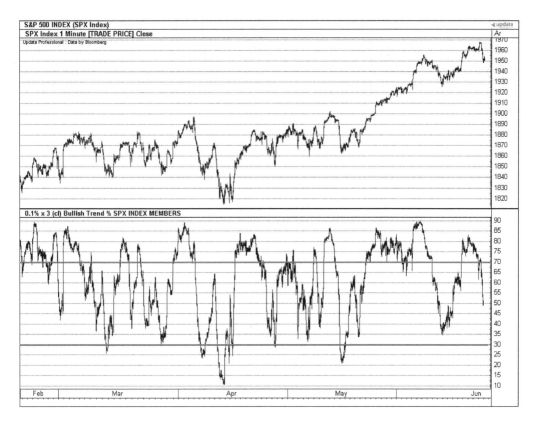

CHART 9-5: 1 MINUTE CHART OF THE S&P 500 WITH 0.1% BULLISH TREND PERCENT OF THE CONSTITUENTS BASED ON 1 MINUTE DATA

OTHER WAYS TO MEASURE MARKET BREADTH

The three market breadth indicators covered in this chapter are unique to Point and Figure charts, meaning that the conditions are based on the Point and Figure charts and therefore not available on time-based charts. It is, however, possible to measure market breadth in some of the ways used on time-based charts and apply those to Point and Figure charts. One such indicator is the percentage of stocks above a moving average. You have already seen that you can draw moving averages on Point and Figure charts, so counting the number of stocks in a universe where the X or O column is above the moving average is possible and gives a valid market breadth indicator. Varying the column length of the moving average alters the time horizon of the indicator, as of course will altering the box size.

SUMMARY

The 21st century has provided two additional Point and Figure-based market breadth indicators to add to the one from the 20th century. They are not substitutes for one another but rather each shows a different time horizon using the same Point and Figure box size. The shortest time horizon is X-Column Percent, which measures the percentage of stocks in an X column; the next is the 20th century's Bullish Percent, which measures the percentage of stocks on double-top buy signals; and the longest time horizon is Bullish Trend Percent, which measures the percentage of stocks in a 45° uptrend.

Bullish Trend Percent helps you with the start of long-term bull markets, which may have a few legs. Bullish Percent helps you to find the start of bull trends within the major bull market signalled by Bullish Trend Percent, and X-Column Percent helps you find additional entry points following small corrections, after Bullish Percent has signalled a bull run.

Market breadth indicators are more about the start of bull markets rather than the end of them. Dips below 30% are excellent buying opportunities but dips above 70% are not selling opportunities – rather they are opportunities to relook at the portfolio and change the composition.

The time horizon of all Point and Figure-based market breadth charts can be altered by reducing the box size without changing the time frame of the data, and further reduced by reducing the time frame of the data, allowing further reduction in the box size.

Because of the developments that include the use of time-based chart tools on Point and Figure charts, it is possible to construct other market breadth indicators based on these, such as the percentage of stocks above the moving average.

Conclusion

POINT AND FIGURE WASN'T DRAGGED KICKING AND SCREAMING into the 21st century – it had already prepared itself for new ideas in the late 20th century. If you have got this far, you will now be aware that there is so much more to Point and Figure charts than you ever thought possible. In the past you would have been aware that trends could be assessed with subjective and 45° trend lines, but in the 21st century moving averages can be used to assess trends on a chart with no time scale. This is exciting for any Point and Figure analyst.

In the past Point and Figure analysis consisted of looking for patterns, observing trends and establishing targets, but the use of calculated tools and indicators has changed all that. Never before has this power existed when analysing a Point and Figure chart. There was never any thought that you could say a Point and Figure chart was overbought or oversold with the aid of an oscillator based on the chart itself. Never before could the price action of a Point and Figure chart be seen to be losing momentum and displaying divergence. Never before could the volume behind a column or at a box price level be used to assess the strength of a move and whether support or resistance is likely to be encountered. All these are now possible in the 21st century. Furthermore, all these tools and indicators can be applied to the Point and Figure analysis of relative strength and spreads.

Although Point and Figure stole some ideas from time-based charts and adapted then for Point and Figure use, it also has its own indicator based purely on the Point and Figure chart, namely the Point & Figure Trend Oscillator. Then, as a gesture of goodwill, it gave the oscillator and 45° trend lines back to time-based analysts so that these can be used to obtain a Point and Figure perspective on non-Point and Figure charts.

Not only have good Point and Figure charts been difficult to find, causing many to abandon them, but with no added analysis they have always been difficult to read. Adding targets and 45° trend lines made it a lot easier, but it was still lacking something. As time-based charts gained more tools and indicators, so they gained supporters, leaving Point and Figure as an unfavoured technique.

The first clue that so much more was possible was the realisation that moving averages could be calculated from and used on a Point and Figure chart. That gave rise to the use of powerful tools such as Bollinger bands, Parabolic SAR and Donchian channels. But it is not restricted to those; literally any tool that was developed for time-based charts can be modified for use on

Point and Figure charts. Then the groundbreaking thought that the logic behind calculating moving averages could be used to calculate and use technical indicators such as MACD, RSI and others has given Point and Figure the power to become the favoured technique of the 21st century. To be able to now look a chart with these tools and indicators is as if someone has turned on the lights.

This is now the third century that Point and Figure has been around. It stood still for much of that time but it has moved into the 21st century with a bang, making it one of the most accurate and popular methods of technical analysis. No right thinking technical analyst can afford to ignore Point and Figure charts now. The old criticisms – pointing at the lack of volume, the inability to measure trends with moving averages, the inability to assess the state of the price with hundreds of indicators – have been cast aside. Point and Figure has overtaken other methods because, as you have seen, there are some techniques which are unique to Point and Figure.

Point and Figure is indeed the chart of the 21st century. There is no doubt, however, that the seeds have been sewn and more new techniques will emerge, some we can't even imagine at this stage. No one in the West had heard of candle charts until Steve Nison exposed them in 1991, and now they are used by every analyst and trader. In a different way, everyone has heard of Point and Figure charts, but not everyone is using them. Hopefully that will change now that their flexibility has been exposed.

It is with that thought that I commend Point and Figure and all these techniques to you and hope that you, like me, will benefit from using them.

Jeremy du Plessis

References and Further Reading

Many fine Technical Analysis books have been written over the years. Listed below are some that have been referred to in this book. You will find many others listed in the bibliography of *The Definitive Guide to Point and Figure*.

Appel, Gerald, *Technical Analysis Power Tools for Active Investors*, Financial Times/Prentice Hall, 1999

Bensignor, Rick (Editor), *New Thinking in Technical Analysis*, Bloomberg Press, Princeton, 2000

Bollinger, John, *Bollinger on Bollinger Bands*, McGraw-Hill, New York, 2001

du Plessis, Jeremy, *The Definitive Guide to Point and Figure*, Harriman House, Petersfield, 2005, 2012

du Plessis, Jeremy, 'Futures and Commodity Contracts – To adjust or not to adjust, that is the question', *STA Market Technician* Issue 77, September 2014

Granville, Joseph, *Granville's New Strategy of Daily Stock Market Timing for Maximum Profit*, Simon & Schuster, 1976

Keller, David (Editor), *Breakthroughs in Technical Analysis*, Bloomberg Press, New York, 2007

Markstein, David, *How to Chart Your Way to Market Profits*, Arco Publishing, New York, 1972

Wilder Jr, J. Welles, *New Concepts in Technical Trading Systems*, Trend Research, Greensboro, NC, 1978

Index

Figures are referenced in italics, charts in bold and notes as 1n2 (page 1 note 2)

THE DEFINITIVE GUIDE TO POINT AND FIGURE

A Comprehensive Guide to the Theory and Practical Use of the Point and Figure Charting Method

Point and Figure charts are one of the great secrets of the Technical Analysis world. Highly sophisticated and with a thoroughbred pedigree, they can, however, be overlooked by traders today. Jeremy du Plessis – one of the foremost Point and Figure experts in the world –returns with a fully updated second edition of this definitive guide in an effort to redress this imbalance.

This second edition, with an extensive revision to the text and introduction of brand new techniques, demystifies the world of Point and Figure charting. It includes a detailed explanation of the history and development of the technique from its invention to the modern day, and covers the makeup of the chart patterns, why they are created, and how to interpret them. Throughout, readers are encouraged to understand Point and Figure charts from first principles, rather than just remember the names of a series of patterns.

Also featured in the second edition are:

- » A step-by-step analysis of the FTSE 100 Index using the 3-box method, as well as the NASDAQ Composite Index, using the 1-box method
  - » A new explanation of how Point and Figure parameters are chosen and the implications of choosing them
    - » Full discussion of Point and Figure gaps and how they provide valuable information about the chart
  - » Price and volume activity histograms and how they provide information about support and resistance

All this is illustrated with numerous colour charts and observations from years of trading experience.

Part of the Market Technicians Association (MTA) Required Reading list.